# POWER
## WALK THROUGH THE
# HOLY SPIRIT

# POWER
## WALK THROUGH THE HOLY SPIRIT

JAMES E. WEBB

*AuthorHouse™ LLC*
*1663 Liberty Drive*
*Bloomington, IN 47403*
*www.authorhouse.com*
*Phone: 1-800-839-8640*



*Published by AuthorHouse 09/25/2013*

*ISBN: 978-1-4918-1596-0 (sc)*
*ISBN: 978-1-4918-1594-6 (hc)*
*ISBN: 978-1-4918-1595-3 (e)*

*Library of Congress Control Number: 2013916615*



*This book is printed on acid-free paper.*

# CONTENTS

# ACKNOWLEDGEMENT

I want to first and foremost thank God the Father who is my Creator, God the Son who is my Savior and God the Holy Spirit who is my Keeper. Without Him and His inspiration and guidance this book would never have been. I also thank Him for "ordering" my words that they might be a help in the ***Power*** walk of believers.

Secondly, I want to thank my family for their support and encouragement in this endeavor. Your sacrifices of time with me, creating an environment around me so that I could hear from the Lord is greatly appreciated.

To my wife, "my cool breeze on a hot day and warm hug on a cold night", Sharon Lavern, I thank God daily for sending you to me. I thank you for being a wife who brings honor to her husband, a mother to our children, a person in whom I can confide and my "best" friend. You have helped me to become the minister that God would have me to be, the husband that I wanted to be, the father that I needed to be and the man that the Master created me to be.

To Donavon and Carmen, thank you for sharing "Daddy" with so many others. I love you both and am extremely proud of you.

I want to say thank you to a special group of individuals who continued to encourage me in the process. Out of fear of overlooking someone who provided me suggestions and insights, I want to express to each of you how appreciative I am for your commentary, corrections, and charity shown toward me.

Last and certainly not least, I want to thank the Bethesda Missionary Baptist Church of Marshall, Texas for you being led by the Holy Spirit to call me as your pastor. Because of your love and support, allowing Bethesda to be a "spiritual racetrack" where ***Power*** walk could be implemented, we have all grown because of the experience.

To all who purchase this book, I say "Thank You". I also greet you as fellow believers and extend words of encouragement as you begin or continue your ***Power*** walk toward spiritual maturity through the aid of the Holy Spirit.

# THE POWER WALKER PLEDGE

You've done it! The decision has been made, the dye has been cast, and you have stepped over the line with an emphatic profession of faith in Jesus Christ. As a disciple of Christ, you have verbally declared that you will no longer look back, let up, slow down, back away, or be stagnant. By faith, your past has been redeemed, your present makes sense, and your eternal future is now secure. By declaration, you are finished with low living, sight walking, worldly talking, miserly giving, and spiritless visions. Because you have given preeminence by Christ, you no longer need prosperity, position, promotions, power, or popularity to be considered a success. By worldly standards, you no longer have to be right, recognized, regarded, or rewarded because you are redeemed by the Resurrected Savior.

Being declared justified, you can live by faith, walk in victory, and labour in love. Your mission is clear and undeniable because it has been conferred by Christ. You cannot be bought, compromised, detoured, lured away, turned back, deluded, or delayed. By the power of the Holy Spirit, you will not flinch in the face of fear, hesitate in the presence of hostility, pander at the pool of popularity, or meander in the maze of mediocrity. As you press toward the mark of the high calling, you will not give up, shut up, or let up, until you have prayed up, praised up, paid up, and spoken up for your Lord and Savior, Jesus Christ.

You've done it! You are an armor wearing, truth proclaiming, sword carrying Power walker. Therefore, **Power walk** in the power of the Holy Spirit! [adapted]

# INTRODUCTION

"Although every believer has the Holy Spirit, it is possible to operate our lives apart from His control."[1]

The athlete that expends a tremendous amount of energy and burns off necessary electrolytes might drink a **Powerade**. An employee with more tenure might pull a **power play** in order to get a preferred promotion or assignment. An electrical short circuit might result in a **power drain**. The Dallas Cowboys of the early 1990s and the Michael Jordan-led Chicago Bulls were considered **powerhouses**. In preparation for a job interview, businessmen might wear a **power tie** or might suggest a **power lunch** to impress the potential client. A fitness conscious female might prefer a **power walk** to a leisure stroll. Although very different, each of these items is a description and the common bond among them is the word, **power**.

The title of this book draws on the same word: "Power!" However, the power that the believer needs to progress

---

1 Raymond McHenry. McHenry's Quips, Quotes & Other Notes. (Peabody, MA: Hendrickson Publishers, 1998), p. 126.

spiritually is the **power** that comes "through the Holy Spirit"[2] (Romans 15:13) and the **walk** is the one that burns off sinful calories and builds biblical muscles. Yet, as McHenry affirmed, it is possible to live our lives apart from the control of the Holy Spirit. His power can lie dormant—available, but not being used, like power stored in a battery. To live and walk victoriously on the **Power walk**, the believer must tap into the effectual power of God that He provides through the Holy Spirit. This book is designed to help believers maintain their spiritual equilibrium and is intended to be informational, inspirational and practical as believers progress toward spiritual maturity, relying on the spiritual elixir which is the power of the Holy Spirit. In the words of Charles C. Ryrie, the author of *The Holy Spirit*, "He is the solution to the problems of every Christian, the antidote for every error, the power for every weakness, the victory for every defeat, the supply for every need, and the answer for every question."[3] The power of the Holy Spirit is readily available to every believer and to fail to tap into it, is to find oneself hamstrung on the **Power walk**.

*Power walk through the Holy Spirit* uses POWER as an acrostic. For those unfamiliar with the word *acrostic,* it is a poem or series of lines in which certain letters, usually the first in each line, read in sequence, form a name, word, motto or message. Other familiar religious acrostics include

---

2 Frank Charles Thompson. The Thompson Chain-Reference Bible (King James Version). (Indianapolis: B. B. Kirkbride Bible Co., 1988), Romans 15:13 KJV (King James Version).

3 Charles C. Ryrie. The Holy Spirit. (Chicago: Moody Press, 1965), p. 11

PUSH—Pray Until Something Happens, JOY—Jesus, Others, You; MASTER—Ministries Anointed for Service through Teamwork, Education & Reformation and STOMP—Striving to Obey the Master's Plan. This POWER acrostic represents five spiritual disciplines in which every believer must become proficient, if spiritual growth is to flourish. They are: **Prayer, Obedience, Worship, Evangelism** and **Reading** the Word of God. These disciplines, which require the empowering presence of the Holy Spirit to be done correctly, are foundational to a believer's **Power walk**.

*Power walk through the Holy Spirit* provides important and helpful guidance concerning the significance of the Holy Spirit in spiritual growth. These disciplines act as fuel to help believers on the **Power** walk finish victoriously. I will deal more fully with the word *power*, but as it relates to the word *walk*, two positive statements come into view, namely "walk in the Spirit" and "be led of the Spirit."[4] Both of these involve a journey where reliance on the Holy Spirit is necessary. Walking in the Spirit guarantees freedom from the flesh, while being led of the Spirit guarantees freedom from the law. *Walk* has been classified as the active side of faith and 'to be led' as the passive side. A successful **Power walk** is thereby predicated on the willingness of believers to walk with and be led by the Holy Spirit, simultaneously. When the believer *walks* in the Spirit, he is stepping out, venturing forth or putting his feet down in faith. When the believer is *led* by the Spirit, he is yielding, following, submitting and

---

[4] Galatians 6:16,18.

surrendering to the promptings of the Spirit. The **Power walk** is challenging, but it is not impossible. If the believer's **Power walk** is to be one that goes from grace to grace and glory to glory, reliance on the power of the Holy Spirit is vital.

*Power walk through the Holy Spirit* will enable believers to understand why the "fervent effectual prayers of the righteous availeth much."[5] **Prayer**, as the reader will see, is not a proliferation of prose or an exercise in alliteration, but a continuous discipline of communication with a holy God. Although there is a how, when, and where of prayer, more importantly, the believer will see the futility of prayer if the Holy Spirit is not intimately involved.

While on the **Power walk**, the question is to obey or not to obey. Obedience is a mandate from God. *Power walk through the Holy Spirit* shows that this mandate is most effectively fulfilled when the believer depends on the Holy Spirit daily. As imperfect "becomings," **Obedience** is not accomplished through "will-power," but through "surrendered will power." **Obedience** provides proof of repentance and evidence of the believer's relationship with God. Self-controlling self will never lead to a victorious **Power walk**. Only as the believer is controlled by the Holy Spirit can true obedience be accomplished.

Then too, there is the discipline of **Worship**. Defined as the human response to the perceived presence of the divine,

---

5 James 5:16.

transcending human activity, worship is a holy endeavor. *Power walk through the Holy Spirit* will help the believer visualize through scripture the igniting force of the Holy Spirit in **Worship**, both private and corporate. **Worship**, which should quicken the conscience, feed the mind, purge the imagination, open the heart, and transform the will of believers, is a Spirit controlled discipline. Believers who participate in Spirit-led worship will experience a closeness to God that will result in inward and outward changes.

With the lost needing to be found and darkness enveloping the souls of those without Jesus Christ, the Good News must be shared. *Power walk through the Holy Spirit* challenges believers to **Evangelize**. Believers must face their fear and realize that unsaved people are not the enemy, but are victims of the enemy. They are in a spiritual headlock by the gods of this world and therefore need someone to help them break free. Additionally, evangelism includes not only the unsaved, but also those converts that have strayed from the safety of the sheepfold, *Power walk through the Holy Spirit* provides some tools that can assist in the believers evangelistic commission. These formulas and methodologies are helpful, but guidance by the Holy Spirit is essential. He, the Holy Spirit, not only goes with the believer, but He precedes the witness, convicts the spiritually blind, and regenerates the heart. This direct order from headquarters, heaven, is not reserved for a select few, but is expected of every believer.

Because the other disciplines are dependent on how well we know God and the power offered to every believer, **Reading** the Word of God is of utmost importance. *Power* *walk through the Holy Spirit* pays special attention to this discipline because of the increase in biblical illiteracy that is plaguing the Christian community. Although no differentiation will be made within the book, it is important to know, you can "read without studying; however," you can never "study without reading." The Bible is the light that guides the way and therefore should be read regularly, repetitively, and reflectively. These three "R's" should be done with a healthy reliance on the Holy Spirit for illumination.

Although not a complete analysis of *pneumatology*, the study of the Holy Spirit, the believer will see why being Spirit filled is so important while on the **Power walk**. His influence on and in believers helps them to better employ the disciplines resulting in vigorous spiritual growth. Therefore, to resist or ignore His help is akin to stripping the necessary nutrients from a sapling.

The power discussed in this book comes from God; and this divine power is available to all believers. In spite of the misconceptions concerning the Holy Spirit and ignorance of His work, a better understanding of the third person of the Trinity is crucial to the believer's spiritual progress. Spiritual enlightenment transforms facts of promise into factors of power. Knowledge of His indwelling presence, life-giving energy, and sanctifying power will equip believers with the necessary tools to remain spiritually upright throughout their **Power walk.** The believers reliance on the Holy Spirit to guide them, results in Triune inspiration and community admiration. It is the will of God that every believer aspires to be "filled with the Spirit."[6]

Power belongs to God and He is at liberty to give it to whom He chooses. In his book, *Holy Spirit Power*, Charles Spurgeon writes: "Power is the special and peculiar prerogative of God and God alone."[7] The Psalmist records, "God has spoken once; twice have I heard this; that power belongs to God."[8] "God is God and power belongs to Him although at times He might sprinkle us with a portion of it." [He] delegates a portion of power to His creatures, yet the power belongs to Him." Man might reign in power for a moment and riches might empower people to honor, but "riches and honor come from [God], and [He] reignest over all; and in [His] hand is power and might . . ."[9] The Leviathans and the Behemoths might glide effortlessly on or through the sea, but it is God who "divideth the sea with His power."[10] The summit of Mount Everest might stretch its snow-capped peaks toward heaven, but "His strength sets fast the mountains."[11] As believers commit themselves to this **Power walk**, they will come face to face with some immoveable objects and some unclimbable mountains. Believers will travel on some dark roads and be drawn down into some dangerous depths. However, through it all, they

---

6 Ephesians 5:18.

7 Charles H. Spurgeon. Holy Spirit Power (New Kensington, PA: Whitaker House, 1996), p. 29.

8 Psalm 62:11.

9 1 Chronicles 29:12.

10 Job 26:12.

11 Psalm 55:6.

must trust in the Irresistible Force and the Illuminating Light who is the Holy Spirit.

The Holy Spirit, according to Paul Jackson in the *Holman Bible Dictionary,* is described as "the mysterious Third Person of the Trinity through whom God acts, reveals His will, empowers individuals, and discloses His personal presence in the Old and New Testament."[12] Furthermore, the Holy Spirit provides the necessary inspiration for all who rely upon His supernatural indwelling and direction. To truly appreciate His work, Paul tells us that the Holy Spirit "works in you both to will and to do"[13] according to God's purpose, enabling His people to fulfill their new, godly desires and that includes the believer's **Power walk**. The Holy Spirit, who is a Person not a personification, plays a pivotal role in this God-ordained **Power walk**. Being a Person, He exhibits intellectual, emotional, and willful attributes as is common to any person. The Holy Spirit can be reverenced,[14] lied to,[15] resisted,[16] obeyed,[17] and outraged.[18]

---

12 Paul Jackson article on The Holy Spirit, Trent C. Butler Holman Bible Dictionary (Nashville: Holman Bible Publishers, 1991), pp. 662,663.

13 Philippians 2:12,13.

14 Psalm 51:11.

15 Acts 5:3.

16 Acts 7:51.

17 Acts 10:19-21.

18 Hebrews 10:29.

He is the same Person who:

- testifies in John 15:26: "But when the Helper comes, whom I shall send to you from the Father, the Spirit of truth who proceeds from the Father, He will testify of Me."
- reproves in John 16:8: "And when [the Holy Spirit] come, He will reprove the world of sin, and of righteousness, and of judgment."
- teaches in John 16:12,13: "I still have many things to say to you, but you cannot bear them now. However, when He, the Spirit of truth, has come, He will guide you into all truth; for He will speak not on His own authority, but whatever He hears He will speak; and He will tell you things to come."
- commands in Acts 8:29: "Then the Spirit said unto Philip, Go near, and join thyself to this chariot."
- separates in Acts 13:2: "As they ministered to the Lord, and fasted, the Spirit said, Separate me Barnabas and Saul for the work whereunto I have called them."
- sends in Acts 13:4: "So they, being sent forth by the Spirit, departed unto Seleucia, and from thence they sailed to Cyprus."
- leads in Romans 8:14: "For as many as are led by the Spirit of God, these are the sons of God."
- intercedes in Romans 8:26: "Likewise the Spirit also helpeth our infirmities: for we know not what we should pray for as we ought: but the Spirit [Himself] maketh intercession for us with groanings which cannot be uttered."
- searches in 1 Corinthians 2:10: "But God has revealed them through His Spirit. For the Spirit searches all things, yes, the deep things of God."

- cries in Galatians 4:6: "And because you are sons, God has sent forth the Spirit of His Son into your hearts, crying out . . .",
- speaks in Revelation 2:7: "He that has an ear, let him hear what the Spirit says to the churches . . ."

It is the author's hope and prayer that *Power walk through the Holy Spirit* will encourage you as you use it as a resource for your personal **Power walk**. May God continue to bless you richly; and remember, if you rely on the Holy Spirit when you start the race toward spiritual maturity, not only will you finish the race, but do so with **POWER!**

# PRAY IN THE SPIRIT

"The power of prayer is not in the one who prays, but in the one who hears it."[1]

"To be a Christian without prayer is no more possible than to be alive without breathing"[2]

"The Lord is near to all who call upon Him, to all who call upon Him in truth."

(Psalm 145: 18)

Have you ever played the game, 'How far?' Its rules are quite simple. You fill up your gas tank and then drive to see how far you can go before you fill up again. You watch the gauge nervously as it gets closer to the big E, hoping that you win by judging correctly. What about your spiritual gas tank? Do you play 'How far' with it while trying to see how far you can get on a single fill-up? One writer said, "Prayer

---

1 Raymond McHenry. McHenry's Quips, Quotes & Other Notes (Peabody, MA: Hendrickson Publishers, 1998); p. 198

2 Joanne Stuart Sloan and Cheryl Sloan-Wray. The Life That Matters (Birmingham, AL: New Hope Publishers, 2002), p. 17

moves the hand that moves the world, and prayer is the only omnipotence God grants to us."[3]

If a believer is going to grow and progress spiritually, he must learn to pray. The focus of prayer should not be on the how, when, and where, but on reliance on the assistance of the Holy Spirit. **Prayer** is the first discipline in the POWER acrostic. As physical exercise makes the body fit and strong, the spiritual exercise of prayer is essential for a healthy spiritual body. By staying "prayed up," believers on the Power walk won't find themselves on empty when spiritual reserves are needed.

J. Oswald Sanders adds this lofty view of prayer:

No spiritual exercise is such a blending of complexity and simplicity. It is the simplest form of speech that infant lips can try, yet the sublimest strains that reach the Majesty on high. It is as appropriate to the aged philosopher as to the little child. It is the ejaculation of a moment and the attitude of a lifetime. It is the expression of the rest of faith and of the fight of faith. It is an agony and an ecstasy. It is submissive and yet importunate. In the one moment it lays hold of God and binds the devil. It can be focused on a single objective and it can roam the world. It can be abject confession and rapt adoration. It invests puny man with a sort of omnipotence (Effective Prayer [Chicago: Moody, 1969], 7).[4]

---

3 Michael Green. Illustrations for Biblical Preaching (Grand Rapids, MI: Baker Book House, 1989), p. 280.

4 MacArthur, J. 1995. Alone with God. Includes indexes. Victor Books: Wheaton, Ill.

Through prayer, one of the primary disciplines for spiritual growth, believers communicate with God. Note that I said communicate rather than legislate. Too many believers pray "with our minds on hold and our mouths on automatic."[5]

Through prayer, believers are able to express their gratitude to God, confess their sins, and come to Him with personal requests. Daniel is one biblical role model for prayer that comes to mind. When one examines his life, he was not only consistent in his prayer life, but he also demonstrated an unshakable faith in God. He was in constant communication with God as evidenced by his praying three times a day (Daniel 6:10)[6], even in enemy territory. Daniel did not wait until he was in trouble or when it was more convenient, but he was willing to send up a prayer unto God at any moment. Believers must learn to do likewise. Prayer is an essential discipline of the Power walk and by relying on the Holy Spirit for direction, the prayers of believers will become more powerful. Richard Foster in his book Celebration of Discipline, states that "prayer catapults [the believer] onto the frontier of the spiritual life and of all the Spiritual Disciplines, prayer is the most central because it ushers us into perpetual communion with the Father."[7] Power walkers must forever remember that prayer is a key ingredient in a

---

5 Ibid, p. 272.

6 "Now when Daniel knew that the writing was signed, he went into his house; and his windows being open in his chamber toward Jerusalem, he kneeled upon his knees three times a day, and prayed, and gave thanks before his God, as he did aforetime."

7 Richard J. Foster. Celebration of Discipline (New York, NY: HarperCollins Publishers, 1978), p. 33.

life that is God pleasing and glorifying. While striving to live a Christ-centered life, don't forget the importance of having a prayer-centered one as well. It has been my experience as a pastor, that many believers depend more on planning than on praying, especially when it comes to spiritual growth. Planning is appropriate, but prayer should come first. Remember, prayer is not the proliferation of prose that pathetically masquerades as prophetic proclamation. Prayer is not the rhythmic alliteration of analytical arguments that captivate the audience. Prayer is not born out of rudimental ritualism that is without power or effectiveness. Prayer is getting in contact with the Lord God and acknowledging ones inability to go it alone.

The spiritual discipline of prayer has been defined as the dialogue between God and people and dialogue is what is important in prayer. Prayer makes a difference in what happens. Oswald Chambers was quoted as saying "It is not so true that 'prayer changes things' as that prayer changes me and I change things."[8] Richard Foster is quoted as saying "to pray is to change."[9] Mother Teresa, who knew the importance of keeping an ear open to the voice of God said, "As blood is to the body, prayer is to the soul, and it brings you closer to God."[10] Randy Hachett states "Our understanding of prayer will correspond to our understanding of God. When God is seen as desiring to bless and sovereignly free to respond to

---

8 Sloan, p. 15.

9 Foster, p. 33.

10 Sloan, p. 26.

persons, then prayer will be seen as dialogue with God."[11] As believers pray, they will be led into a greater communion with God, and a greater understanding of His will.

Is prayer important? The answer is a resounding "Yes!" In fact for the believer on his or her Power walk toward spiritual maturity, that question is akin to asking if water is wet or ice cold. Not only is it important, but according to R. C. Sproul, in his book Five Things Every Christian Needs To Grow, "it is our duty, our privilege and a powerful means of grace."[12] It is crystal clear from Scripture, both Old and New Testament, that God's people are called to be people of prayer. Too frequently in the modern-day church, there is a greater concern for people of God being pay-ers instead of pray-ers. While on the Power walk, prayer needs to be done consistently and persistently, but most of all faithfully. By becoming a powerful pray-er, the Power walk will yield greater spiritual rewards.

Is prayer important? C. H. Spurgeon said, "Prayer pulls the rope down below and the great bell rings above the ears of God. Some scarcely stir the bell, for they pray languidly; others give only an occasional jerk at the rope. He who communicates with heaven is the man who grasps the rope boldly and pulls continuously with all his might."[13]

---

[11] Randy Hatchett article on Prayer, Butler, p. 1132

[12] R. C. Sproul. Five Things Every Christian Needs To Grow (Nashville: W. Publishing Group, 2002), p. 24.

[13] Green, p. 273.

To properly communicate with God through prayer, believers must make sure they are in communion with Him. When there is a breakdown in communion, there tends to be a breakdown in communication. A Power walker must not take his or her relationship with Christ for granted. Talk to Him daily that your communion is not jeopardized or walk threatened.

Is prayer important? The word prayer or the root word pray is mentioned approximately 522 times in the Bible.[14] Matthew declares, "Ask, and it shall be given unto you; seek, and you shall find; knock, and it shall be opened unto you" (Matthew 7:7). The physician Luke says, " . . . men ought always to pray, and not faint" (Luke 18: 1). Jesus encourages the believer to " . . . Ask, and ye shall receive, that your joy may be full" (John 16: 24). Paul told the church at Rome to " . . . [rejoice] in hope, [be] patient in tribulation, continuously [steadfast] in prayer" (Romans 12:12) He told the church at Corinth "Defraud ye not one the other, except it be with consent for a time, that ye may give yourselves to fasting and prayer . . ." (1 Corinthians 7:5). He told the believers at Philippi to "Be careful for nothing; but in everything by prayer and supplication with thanksgiving let your requests be made known unto God" (Philippians 4:6) Paul emphasizes the importance of praying in the Spirit when he said, "Praying always with all prayer and supplication

---

14 Franklin Holy Bible Electronic King James Version (Bookman II Model KJV-1440. Burlington, NJ: Franklin Electronic Publishers, 1999).

in the Spirit . . ." (Ephesians 6: 18). Paul also said to "Pray without ceasing" (I Thessalonians 5:17).

Is prayer important? If Jesus did it and He was God in the flesh, would you think that prayer is important? Scripture reveals that Jesus made prayer a priority in His life. You will find Jesus praying at His baptism.[15] Jesus can be seen praying before He chose the Twelve.[16] When the crowds began to increase Jesus prayed.[17] Even at His own Transfiguration He can be found praying.[18]

Jesus was a morning pray-er. Mark 1:35 tells us that " . . . in the morning, rising up a great while before day, He went out, and departed into a solitary place, and there prayed." Jesus was an evening pray-er. According to the gospel of Mark, " . . . when He had sent them away, He departed into a mountain to pray" (Mark 6: 46). Jesus even pulled some all-night prayer sessions, as seen in Luke 6:12, "And it came to pass in those days, that He went out into a mountain to pray, and continued all night in prayer to God" (Luke 6: 12). To successfully finish the Power walk, believers must spend quality time with God in prayer. Whenever spiritual fatigue is being felt, check your prayer gauge. It might be running on empty.

The preceding scriptures remind believers that prayer is one of the essential disciplines of spiritual growth. It is the

---

15 Luke 3:21.

16 Luke 6:12,13.

17 Luke 5:15,16.

18 Luke 9:29.

communication channel between God and believers. John Piper said, in his book Let the Nations be Glad, "Prayer is primarily a wartime walkie-talkie [as believers battles against] the powers of darkness and unbelief and not a domestic intercom to call upstairs for a more comfortable den."[19] As believers give themselves to seeking the guidance of God in prayer, it will become a habit that will soon have you.[20] Many believers have developed the terrible habit of failing to pray. As believers commune with God in prayer, they tap into the power of the Holy Spirit to accomplish the impossible. This power is made accessible to believers, not because of what they do or say, but because of the One who has been given to them, the Holy Spirit. By relying on the Holy Spirit, "praying without ceasing" will become habitual and effectual.

Prayer has always been the means by which the children of God draw closer to him. This is why the disciples asked Jesus to teach them to pray.[21] They did not ask Him to teach them how, but to teach them to pray. Taking some liberties with the word *to*, believers must never get so busy that they forget *to* pray. When there is more sunshine in your life then rain, don't forget *to* pray. When circumstances bring trials and tribulations, don't forget *to* pray. D. L. Moody once

---

19 John Piper. Let the Nations be Glad! (Grand Rapids, MI: Baker Book House, 1993), p. 41.

20 Ibid, pp. 57-62. In this section of the book, we see how the chosen of God sought Him in everything.

21 Luke 11:1.

said "Behind every work of God you will always find some kneeling form."[22]

On my own Power walk, there have been times that the devil was victorious throughout the day because of my failure to fill up with prayer. In my haste to get my day started, I carelessly failed to stop to talk with God. As the day wore on, I felt agitated, discouraged, and defeated. I suffered multiple false starts because of my failure to pause and ask God to guide me through the day. I was powerless in a power hungry world. Having traveled some additional miles on my Power walk, I have learned that prayer prepares the way for a prepared day. An effective prayer life is the provision for every need and the solution for every problem that believers might face on their Power walk.

Prayer has a formula, but it is also a process. Jesus, the greatest example of a powerful pray-er, gave the believer both in the model prayer.[23] Within this model, believers have some guiding principles to assist them through prayer. Alvin Reed, in his book Introduction to Evangelism, outlines these key components of prayer. Using the model prayer as an example, believers find praise, thanksgiving, confession, intercession and petition as key elements of the prayer formula. In addition to those listening and consecration should be included. Prayer that encompasses all of the elements will usher believers to the very throne room of God and as a result two-way communication will take place.

---

22 McHenry, p. 195.

23 Matthew 6:9-13.

Praise is the believer's response to the person of God. Thanksgiving is the believer's response to the goodness of God. Confession is the believer's response to the holiness of God. Intercession is the believer's response to the love of God in desiring to know His will for his life. Petition is the believer's response to the love of God for us. Listening is the believer's response to the voice of God as He speaks to him or her. As believers pray, they should be acutely aware of the voice of God. He is constantly speaking to believers, but He won't raise His voice. Finally, consecration is a believer's prayer of commitment to God.[24]

As believers begin or continue their Power walk, it is vitally important to know as much about prayer and how to do it as effectively as possible. A good place to start would be to read a book on prayer, or study the men and women of prayer as mentioned in the Bible. Another tool that can be used is a model for prayer. A model can jump start your prayer life. A model that comes highly recommended is the ACTS Model. This model is simplistic in context and helpful in direction, but believers must be led by the Holy Spirit, or else prayer will become an exercise in futility. The ACTS System, which consists of four primary components can be helpful for the neophyte or the seasoned pray-er. ACTS is an acrostic that stands for Adoration, Confession, Thanksgiving, and Supplication. Followed with a sincere heart and a contrite

---

[24] Alvin Reid. Introduction to Evangelism (Nashville, TN: Broadman & Holman Publishers, 1998), pp. 142-144.

spirit, this model can jettison the believer to the very throne of God.

Taking a short detour from our look at prayer, most are moved and encouraged by "Faith's Hall of Fame" that the author of Hebrews records in chapter 11 of the book. There exists a catalogue of heroic acts of biblical men and women of faith. R. C Sproul, in his book *Following Christ*, states that although there is not a similar list for the heroes of prayer, such a list could easily be complied. Using the same format of the writer of Hebrews, we can see some remarkable accomplishments by prayer warriors of the Bible.

- By prayer, Esau's heart was changed toward Jacob, so that they met in a friendly, rather than hostile, manner (Genesis 33);
- By the prayer of Moses, God brought the plagues upon Egypt and then removed them again (Exodus 7-11);
- By prayer, Joshua made the sun stand still (Joshua 10);
- By prayer, when Samson was ready to perish with thirst, God brought water out of a hollow place for his sustenance (Judges 15);
- By prayer, Elijah held back the rains for three and one half years. And then by prayer, caused it to rain again (1 Kings 17,18);
- By the prayer of Hezekiah, God sent an angel and killed in one night 185,000 men in Sennacherib's army (2 Kings 19); and,
- By the prayer of Asa, God confounded the army of Zerah (2 Chronicles 14).[1]

---

1 R. C. Sproul. Following Christ (Wheaton, IL: Tyndale House Publishers, 1996, c1991).

The power of prayer on the Power walk is not limited to this partial list. Abraham prayed and received a son in his old age; Moses prayed and God made a highway out of no way at the Red Sea; David escaped the treachery of Saul by prayer; Solomon prayed for great wisdom and received it; Hannah prayed for a man child and begot Samuel and Daniel received the ability to interpret dreams after praying. Through the fervent prayers of the righteous, people have been delivered from peril, healed of diseases, and witnessed innumerable miracles. There is power in prayer and the believer on the Power walk must continuously tap into this power.

Getting back on track concerning the recommendation of studying the prayers of men and women in the Bible, let's consider four: the prayer's of Jabez, David, Peter, and one of my personal favorites, Psalm 5.

If a believer has desires that are within the will of God, the prayer of Jabez is an effective model to study: "And Jabez called on the God of Israel, saying, Oh that thou wouldest bless me indeed, and enlarge my coast, and that thine hand might be with me and that thou wouldest keep me from evil, that it may not grieve me! . . ."[2]

If a believer has sinned against God and communion has been severed, David's prayer for mercy and forgiveness can be profitable: "Have mercy upon me, O God, according to thy loving kindness: According unto the multitude of thy tender mercies blot out my transgressions. Wash me thoroughly

---

2 I Chronicles 4:10.

from mine iniquity, and cleanse me from my sin. For I acknowledge my transgressions: and my sin is ever before me. Create in me a clean heart, O God; and renew a right spirit within me. Cast me not away from thy presence; and take not thy Holy Spirit from me. Restore unto me the joy of thy salvation; and uphold me with thy free spirit."[3]

If a believer is in a life threatening predicament as a result of taking his or her eyes off Jesus, Peter's emergency or "flash" prayer is appropriate; "Lord, save me."[4] In Psalm 5, David prays for guidance from God. I find this prayer energizing in the morning. For it should be the goal of every believer to be guided throughout the day and to feel a connection between you and your heavenly Father.

Throughout the Bible, believers can find strength for the Power walk from the prayers of Spirit-filled men and women of God. Some other notable prayers, besides the ones mentioned above are:

- The prayer of Abraham for Sodom (Genesis 18:23)
- The prayer of Jacob at Penile (Genesis 32:24)
- The prayer of Solomon at Gibeon (I Kings 3:6)
- The prayer of Ezra for the sins of the people (Ezra 9:6)
- The prayer of Habakkuk (Habakkuk 3:1)
- The prayer of the Publican (Luke 18:13)
- The prayer of the dying thief (Luke 23:42)
- The prayer of Paul for the Ephesians (Ephesians 3:14-21)

---

3 Psalm 51:1-3; 10-12.

4 Matthew 14:30.

- The Intercessory prayer of Jesus (John 17), my personal favorite.

R. C. Sproul said, and I am in agreement with him, "Whether you use the Model Prayer . . . ACTS, or something else altogether, the important thing is that you pray."[5] As believers progress on the Power walk and toward spiritual maturity, God promises to be near to all who come to Him in prayer. Prayers are answered through the power of His Spirit. The fullness of the spiritual life is accomplished through the power of the Holy Spirit. Therefore, it is vital that this first discipline of the POWER acrostic— Prayer, be taken seriously: "Pray without ceasing."[6] St. Augustine declares, "For your desire is your prayer; and your desire is without ceasing; your prayer will also be without ceasing."[7]

---

5 Sproul, Five Things Every Christian Needs To Grow, p.40.

6 1 Thessalonians 5:17.

7 Green, p. 280.

## MAKING PRAYER WORK ON THE POWER WALK

- Ask God to give you the desire to pray.
- Study the prayers mentioned in this chapter, as well as others within the Bible.
- Begin keeping a prayer journal. Write down your prayer and the answer to it when it comes.
- Read a book on prayer (recommendations listed below).
- Pray daily about a sinful habit that you need the help of God to overcome.
- Make meditation and fasting a part of your prayer life.
- Get involved in the prayer ministry at your church.
- Experiment with different approaches to prayer.

## PRAYER BOOK RECOMMENDATIONS


- Arthur, Kay. *Lord Teach Me to Pray in 28 Days.* Eugene, OR: Harvest House Publishers, 2001.
- Copeland, Germaine. *Prayers That Avail Much.* Tulsa, OK: Harrison House, Inc., 1999.
- Donihue, Anita C. *When I'm on My Knees.* Uhrichsville, OH: Barbour Publishing, Inc., 1997
- Hanegraaff, Hank. *The Prayer of Jesus.* Nashville: Word Publishing Group, 2001.
- Torrey, R. A. *How to Pray.* New Kensington, PA: Whitaker House, 1993.

# OBEY IN THE SPIRIT

"Nothing is as provoking to God as disobedience, setting up our wills in competition with His."[8]

"If you love me, keep my commandments." (St. John 14: 15)

"Be ye doers of the word, and not hearers only, deceiving your own selves."

What kind of hearer are you when it comes to the Word of God? Are you an apathetic hearer who hears the Word but aren't prepared to receive or understand it? Are you a superficial hearer who is temporarily affected by what you have heard, but don't allow it to take root in your heart? Or maybe you are a preoccupied hearer who receives the Word but let worries of the world and fleshly desires choke it out? Or maybe you are what James calls a reproducing hearer; one who receives the Word, understands the Word, and then allows it to take root in the heart thereby allowing fruit to spring forth from a receptive heart. To become spiritually mature, believers must be committed to becoming good hearers and doers of the Word; they must be attentive to the details provided by God through His Word,

---

8 Sloan, p. 143

and they must prefer the "authorized" standard instead of the "reversed" (doing the opposite of what Scripture says) standard version of the Bible. "But be ye doers of the word, and not hearers only, deceiving your own selves."

The second discipline of the **POWER** acrostic that believers need to incorporate into their **Power walk** toward spiritual maturity is **Obedience**. If there was ever a single discipline that believers need the power of the Holy Spirit to accomplish, then **Obedience** is the one because man is disobedient by nature. If you find that statement to be a stretch, then tell me, "Have you ever had to teach a child how to be bad?"

R. A. Torrey once said, "Power is lost through self-indulgence. The one who would have God's power must lead a life of self-denial." Obedience is not automatic; it takes sincere effort. Obedience is an expression of the believer's love for God, who he or she now calls Father. In fact, "He that has the commandments of the Lord and keeps them, he it is that loves the Lord."[9] Jesus straightforwardly tells believers that obedience and love go hand in hand. It is more than lovely words; it is commitment and conduct. Because of the nature of man, believers don't have the strength to obey without some divine assistance. This is the specific reason the Holy Spirit was given. As believers yield themselves to God, they are provided the necessary power to **Power walk** in obedience.

---

[9] John 14:21.

As believers try to pace themselves, they must keep in focus the need of wholehearted obedience. On the **Power walk**, believers must be careful not to exhibit an obedience that could be labeled *a la carte*. "This day the Lord thy God hath commanded thee to do these statutes and judgments; thou therefore keep and do them with all thine heart, and with all thy soul."[1] A believer cannot merely render lip service when obedience is commanded. He or she must be totally sold out to the idea. The believer must continuously and daily rely on the power of the Holy Spirit. Obeying God wholeheartedly can be the difference between life and death. Take as an example Lot's wife, who we are told to remember.[2] Because she chose to disobey what God had told her to the letter,[3] she was judged immediately. Although she departed Sodom in appearance, her heart was still longing for the things of the city. Because of her disobedience, she experienced a fatal failure. Obedience to God must be a priority for every believer.

Likewise, a believer's obedience is the price of spiritual success. Joshua, after Moses had died, had to decide if he would be obedient or not. His success as a spiritual leader would be directly related to his obedience to the leading of

---

1 Deuteronomy 26:16.

2 Luke 17:32 "Remember Lot's wife."

3 Genesis 19:17 "And it came to pass, when they had brought them forth abroad, that he said, Escape for thy life; look not behind thee, neither stay thou in all the plain; escape to the mountain, lest thou be consumed."

God. "This book of the law shall not depart out of thy mouth; but thou shalt meditate therein day and night, that thou mayest observe to do according to all that is written therein: for then thou shalt make thy way prosperous, and then thou shalt have good success."[4] Spiritual success is not an accident. Success comes to those who properly prepare for it. Joshua's success, as is the success of believers, is not predicated on position, prestige, or personal influence, but on being obedient to the expressed Word of God. In the world in which we live, the proclamation "might makes right" is adhered to by the masses. But, a successful Power walk is not achieved by might, but by right. Joshua went down in history as a spiritual millionaire, not because of his position with man, but because of his obedience to God. The difference between glorying in spiritual prosperity and finding oneself spiritually bankrupt depends largely on your obedience to God.

Furthermore, a believer's obedience secures entrance into God's kingdom. There are those who claim obedience in word, but their lives run counter to their claim. They are like clouds that promise rain to a parched earth but yield none, or a brook that promises sweet water only to be found bitter. "Not every one that saith unto me, Lord, Lord, shall enter into the kingdom of heaven; but he that doeth the will of my Father which is in heaven."[5] There are both professors and possessors on this walk that the believer is called to take. Profession of faith in Jesus Christ is what the believer needs

---

4 Joshua 1:8.

5 Matthew 7:21.

to ensure entrance into the kingdom of heaven, but we give "full proof" of our profession when we become obedient followers of Christ, possessors of the Good News. Good intentions will not get us into the kingdom of God nor will they make for a successful **Power walk**. We must show our worthiness, not being ashamed at the day of judgment, by doing what God has commanded.

Lastly, a believer's obedience is the imperative duty of life. Obedience is not something extra that God expects believers to do; it is their duty. Just as a servant who is expected to obey his master due to ownership and respect of authority, so, too, does God expect his children to obey Him. "Then Peter and the other apostles answered and said, We ought to obey God rather than men."[6] (Acts 5: 29). As believers we are "bought with a price" (1 Corinthians 6:20) and therefore are duty bound to obey the One who purchased us with His blood. Because of our being purchased by the shed blood of Jesus Christ, we have an obligation to God and that is obedience. People who commit themselves to God through Jesus Christ, are disassociating themselves from their former boss, the world, and are placing their faith in another. Having done so, they are expected to obey their new Boss. As a result of the believer's profession of faith in Jesus Christ, he or she now belongs to a new Master. As servants, believers are to "obey in all things . . . not according to the flesh; not with

---

6 Acts 5:29.

eye-service, as men pleasers; but in singleness of heart, fearing God."[7]

Again, I reiterate the fact that **Obedience** is not easy because the one with whom believers wrestle on the Power walk is not "flesh and blood,"[8] but spirit. Paul said, "For I know that in me (that is in my flesh) dwelleth no good thing: for to will is present with me; but how to perform that which is good I find not. For the good that I would I do not: but evil which I would not, that I do."[9] That is the primary reason why believers need the power of the Holy Spirit. Although believers might have good intentions, good intentions will not defeat a spiritual enemy. "The devil made me do it" made Flip Wilson famous, but it is a poor excuse for the believer on a Power walk. The devil might play an enticing role in the believer's disobedience; but he cannot make the believer do anything. Ultimately each believer is responsible for his or her actions. A biblical character that was swallowed up by Satan was Jonah. Instead of being obedient to the command of God, he went in the opposite direction.[10] Simply because Satan caused him to be swallowed up by prejudice, he wanted the Ninevites to feel the wrath of God,[11] instead of tasting of His mercy. From his precarious journey, believers should learn that it is better to obey immediately before rationalization takes root. The way of obedience has and will

---

7 Colossians 3:22.

8 Ephesians 6:12.

9 Romans 7:18,19.

10 Jonah 1:3.

11 Jonah 4:2.

always be the way of blessing. Believers are to be quick to hear, but quicker to heed.

With Jonah as proof, without the Holy Spirit, the believer's **Power walk** is doomed for defeat. However, by relying on the Holy Spirit, believers will be suited up and prepared for the spiritual battle that rages within.

The Holy Spirit is the One who guides, protects, elevates, compels, and clothes believers to have a victorious **Power walk**. By depending on the Holy Spirit, believers are able to withstand the tricks of the devil and walk after the way of righteousness and to abhor evil. As believers battle to stay upright and on the right path, they must fight with the power of the Holy Spirit who is "able to keep [them] from falling." (Jude 24). If the believer falls, he has the assurance that he "shall not be utterly cast down" (Psalm 37: 24). Before we proceed, I want to draw your attention to the use of the word "He" and "Him." "Even the Spirit of truth; whom the world cannot receive, because it seeth not, neither knoweth him: but ye know him; for he dwelleth with you, and shall be in you." (John 14:17). For too long we have been addressing the Holy Spirit as "it", either consciously or unconsciously; but we can no more call Him an "it" as we can call God the Father or God the Son an "it". The Holy Spirit is the third Person in the Trinity and He deserves our utmost respect. To deny His Personhood is to deny His real existence. He has been called the "exerted energy of God"[12] in an effort to declassify Him

---

12 Charles C. Ryrie. The Holy Spirit (Chicago, IL: Moody Press, 1965), p. 13.

as Deity. God the Father, God the Son, and God the Holy Spirit make up the Trinity and share in Personhood qualities.

Most look at God as being omnipotent, omnipresent, and omniscient. What then says the Scriptures about the Holy Spirit? The Bible declares that the Holy Spirit is omnipotent: "The Spirit of God hath made me, and the breath of the Almighty have given me life" (Job 33:4). The Bible also verifies His omnipresence: "Whither shall I go from thy Spirit? Or whither shall I flee from thy presence?" (Psalm 139:7). There is also biblical support to His omniscience: "For what man knoweth the things of man, save the spirit of man which is in him? Even so the things of God knoweth no man, but the Spirit of God" (1 Corinthians 2:11). If believers are to fully appreciate the work of the Holy Spirit, they must address Him properly.

The power to obey cannot be found in the created man, but in the Creator of man. I do recall that God did have a conversation with Himself and said "Let us make man" and if He can make man, He can most assuredly help man obey what He has declared. In the **Power walk** that a believer is called to take, there will be times when obedience appears impossible or it puts you in the minority, but be of good courage because if you are in the will of God, you are always in the majority.

The believer is capable of obeying the commands of God through the power of the Holy Spirit as is evident by Biblical witnesses who were tempted toward disobedience but stood fast in their faith in God. Note the following examples:

- Noah in Genesis 6: 22: "Thus did Noah; according to all that God commanded him, so did he."
- Abraham in Genesis 22: 2: "And he said, Take now thy son, thine only son Isaac whom thou lovest, and get thee into the land of Moriah; and offer him there for a burnt offering, and [Abraham] rose up and went unto the place of which God had told him."
- Bezaleel in Exodus 36: 1: "Then wrought Bezaleel and Aholiah, and every wise hearted man, whom the Lord put wisdom and understanding to know how to work all manner of work for the service of the sanctuary, according to all that the Lord had commanded."
- Joshua in Joshua 11: 15: "As the Lord commanded Moses his servant, so did Moses command Joshua and so did Joshua; he left nothing undone of all that the Lord had commanded Moses."
- Hezekiah in II Kings 18: 6: "For he claved to the Lord, and departed not from following him, but kept his commandments, which the Lord commanded Moses."
- Joseph and Mary, the mother of Jesus in Luke 2: 39: "And when they had performed all things according to the law of the Lord . . . ."
- Paul in Acts 26: 19: "Whereupon, O king Agrippa, I was not disobedient unto the heavenly vision."
- Christ in Hebrews 5: 8: "Though he were a Son, yet learned he Obedience by the things which he suffered."

Selective obedience is not obedience at all; it is merely convenience. If believers are to progress spiritually and not develop some spiritual sprained ankles on the **POWER**

**walk**, they must learn to depend on the Holy Spirit, "commit yourself in all thy ways" and "fear God and keep His commandments" (Ecclesiastes 12: 13), which is the whole duty of man. As believers obey the commands of God, the Holy Spirit will guide them into a stronger relationship with God.

Corrie ten Boom said regarding the guidance of the Holy Spirit, "He will guide us by His Spirit if we ask Him to do so, if we are submissive to Him and refuse to be led by our own wisdom."[13] The discipline of guidance is closely tied to the discipline of Obedience. As God guides the believer by His Spirit, the proper response is obedience. Obedience involves obeying God in all areas of the believer's life. This second discipline of the **POWER** *acrostic*—**Obedience**, must have the believer's total commitment if he or she is going to reach the pinnacle of spiritual maturity. The whole issue of this discipline can be summed up with this statement: the best proof of a believer's love for God is obedience. Nothing more . . . nothing less . . . nothing else.

---

[13] Sloan, p. 136.

## OBEDIENCE ON THE POWER WALK

- Study the history of Israel or one of the patriarchs, Abraham, Isaac, Jacob, and observe how obedience or disobedience affected them. Look for the negatives of disobedience and the positives of obedience.
- Study the life of Jesus in the Gospels and how He was obedient to His Father.
- Ask God to help you to obey His commands as they are spelled out in Scripture. When Scripture uncovers an area in your life that God has not been guiding you in, repent and commit yourself to being led by the Spirit.
- Keep a journal to track your progress in the areas that you have placed under the Spirit's guidance. Keep track of times when you yielded to the flesh and journal the cause of the disobedience. Habits can be broken if patterns are discovered.

# WORSHIP IN THE SPIRIT

"To worship is to quicken the conscience by the holiness of God, to feed the mind with the truth of God, to purge the imagination by the beauty of God, to open the heart to the love of God, to devote the will to the purpose of God."[14]

"God is Spirit; and they that worship Him must worship him in spirit and in truth."

(St. John 4: 24).

There is a great lesson to be learned from the dictionary. When things start going badly, we often fear they will only get worse. It seems the *worse* will take us to the *worst*. To prevent the *worse* from advancing into the *worst*, God provides a unique setup within the English language. Any standard dictionary will separate the words, *worse* and *worst,* with the special word, *worship*,[15] a word that comes from the

---

14 Foster, p. 158.

15 Sol Steinmetz, ed. Random House Webster Dictionary (New York: Random House, 1993).

old English "worth-ship," which means to ascribe worth or value to something or someone.[1]

As believers make progress on their **POWER walk**, they must learn how to worship God. Since "God is Spirit"[2], and who can know the mind of God but God, believers must rely on His Spirit to lead them in their worship. Richard Foster said, "To worship is to experience reality, to touch life. Worship is the human response to the divine initiative as well as our response to the overtures of love from the heart of the Father."[3] In order for believers to worship "in Spirit and truth," their worship must be ignited by the divine fire that comes from the Holy Spirit.

The third discipline of the **POWER** acrostic is **Worship**. **Worship** can be defined as "the human response to the perceived presence of the divine, a presence which transcends normal human activity and is holy.[4] It is the due response of man to the self-realization of the Creator, Savior and Lord. Worship is more importantly the distinct and differentiating characteristic between mankind and the animal kingdom. Animals don't worship, they just exist. They have no sense of eternity. In contrast, humans have eternity in their hearts, it having been planted there by God at creation.[5] The devotion of believers on their Power walk is verified and strengthened

---

1 Greg Laurie, New Believer's Guide to Effective Living (Wheaton, Ill. Tyndale House Publishers, Inc.) p. 83.

2 John 4:24 KJV

3 Foster, p. 158.

4 Marvin E. Tate article on Worship, Butler, pp. 1421,1422.

5 Ecclesiastes 3:11.

as they become involved in continuous worship to the One who saved and claimed. Through private and corporate worship, believers should feel the presence of the Holy Spirit working through them, making them more like God who is Spirit. Richard Foster states that "if worship does not change us, it has not been worship."[6]

The worship experience is not one special occasion or event; it is continuous. The word *continuous* speaks of going on without stopping or interruption. It speaks out of the bowels of the Psalmist who declares, "I will bless the Lord at all times, His praise shall continuously be in my mouth."[7] As believers, we should show reverence to God wherever we go and in everything we do. In John 4, a woman at a well was more concerned with the *where* of worship instead of the *why* of worship. Like many today, the problem is not the physical exercise of worship; the problem is the spiritual connection of worship. Many worship in *body*, but not in Spirit. Only worship that is pleasing and acceptable to God, can be classified as true worship. True worship acknowledges the true God. The triune God who is holy, righteous, good, fair, and loving desires the worship of His people. Worship that is true doesn't attempt to transform Him into our image, deciding which attributes we want to keep or toss, but transforms the believer into the image He wants us to be.

**Worship** that is "in Spirit" is worship that comes from a heart that has been renewed by the power of the Holy

---

6 Green, p. 280.

7 Psalm 34:1 KJV

Spirit. No rituals, ceremonies, or devotional formalities can be classified as Spirit-led worship if there is not a willing heart. Warren Wiersbe writes: "The important thing is that we keep the right balance. There is today such an emphasis on Bible knowledge that we are in danger of ignoring, or even opposing, personal experience. While we must not base our theology on experience, neither must we debase our theology by divorcing it from experience. If true worship is the response of the whole person to God, then we dare not neglect the emotions.[8] Relying on the Spirit of God will provide believers with the blessed assurance that God is inhabiting their praise. As the Holy Spirit gives utterance, believers are able to glorify His name through their worship. Gordon Dahl once observed that the biggest hindrance for believers is, "we worship our work, work at our play, and play at our worship."[9]

As expressed by William L. Thrasher, Jr., in his book *Basics for Believers*, one of the interesting truths about the exercise of **Worship** is that God has so ordered it that "we become like the things we worship."[10] If believers focus their eyes, thoughts, and body on the things of the world, then they will become like the idols they worship. If believers worship success, sex, fame, drugs, pleasure, materialism, intellectualism, or independence, then they will become consumed by these vices and make them their god. However,

---

8 Laurie, pp. 86,87.

9 McHenry, p. 280.

10 William L. Thrasher Jr. Basics for Believers (Chicago, IL: Moody Press, 1998), p. 56.

when believers give the Lord the glory He deserves and commit themselves to actions that reflect the indwelling of the Holy Spirit, true worship of God will take place. Believers that guard their hearts and minds in the discipline of Worship and rely on the power of the Holy Spirit, will find themselves in the midst of true worship.

As it relates to the two types of worship, private and corporate, they are interdependent of each other and totally dependent on the Holy Spirit. Private worship can take many forms—prayers, confessions, silence and meditative experiences. These are all types of worship that bring the believer into the consciousness of a perceived holy communion with God. The object of a believer's worship should be God, who has no equal. The Bible declares, "You shall worship the Lord your God and Him only shall you serve."[11] Therefore, worship requires preparation. Believers cannot walk unworthily throughout the day, then magically be able to have Spirit-filled worship. **Worship** requires believers to be sanitized of evil, separated from the world, and sanctified by the Holy Spirit.

Worship is important not only because it is mentioned positively one-hundred and ninety-two times in the Bible,[12] but also because God commands it of believers. Note the examples that support this idea:

---

[11] Matthew 4:10.

[12] Franklin Holy Bible Electronic KJV.

- "And now, behold I have brought the firstfruits of the land, which thou, O Lord, hast given me. And thou shalt set it before the Lord thy God, and worship before the Lord thy God" (Deuteronomy 26: 10).
- "Give unto the Lord the glory due unto his name: bring an offering, and come before him: worship the Lord in the beauty of holiness" (I Chronicles 16: 29).
- "O come, let us worship the Lord in the beauty of holiness: fear before him, all the earth" (Psalm 96: 9).
- "Then saith Jesus unto him, Get thee hence, Satan: for it is written, Thou shalt worship the Lord thy God, and him only shalt thou serve" (Matthew 4: 10).
- " . . . Fear God, and give glory to him; for the hour of his judgment is come: and worship him that made heaven, and earth, and the sea, and the fountains of water" (Revelation 14: 7).

It was God that saved believers from the "hand of the enemy,"[13] and therefore He is worthy of praise and worship. How grateful are you that you have been numbered among the elect of God? How happy are you that your name is in the "lamb's Book of Life?" How relieved are you that you will be counted among the "sheep" and not the "goats?" How blessed will you be when you are *taken* and not *left*?[14] Appreciation for salvation should reveal itself through worship, with the Holy Spirit serving as the Conductor.

---

13 Luke 1:74.

14 See Luke 17:20-37 for more information about the above mentioned idea.

Consider the certain leper who was numbered among the ten,[15] who having been healed as he went, stopped, turned around and went and worshipped Jesus for what He had done. Remember the blind beggar who received his sight,[16] who having his sight restored, could not hold his peace and initiated a praise and worship service among the people. Don't forget the certain lame man who lay at the gate of the temple called Beautiful, daily asking alms,[17] having been made whole got up and went into the temple, walking, leaping and praising God.[18] As a believer, because of the graciousness of God toward you, worship should spring up out of your soul, but to do so correctly is to rely totally on the power of the Holy Spirit. When was the last time you had a private worship service with the Lord? No choir! No musical instruments! No order of service! No sermon! Just you and God! David, a man after God's own heart, did it frequently. In Psalm 66, having cleansed himself by confession, he came to God with a pure heart and called out to God in praise. When believers come to God with a pure heart, God will listen and He will inhabit the praise.

Not only must believers have private worship services, but they are also instructed to routinely come together in corporate worship as well: "not forsaking the assembling of ourselves together, as the manner of some *is*; but

---

15 Luke 17:11-17.

16 Luke 18:35-43.

17 Acts 3:2.

18 Acts 3:8.

exhorting one another: and so much more, as ye see the day approaching."[19]

I can hear someone saying, "I don't need to go to church, especially since God is omnipresent. Besides, the church has too many "hypocrites." Those things might be true, but to disobey a direct order from headquarters regarding corporate worship, is to put in question one's proficiency of the discipline of **Obedience**. Besides, going to a place of worship is beneficial. The church provides encouragement and love to believers. The church allows believers, especially those young in the faith, to learn from more mature Christians. Likewise, the church helps you to discern truth from error. The church also prepares believers for the return of Christ. Hypocritical behavior of the parts or God's omnipresence is no excuse to forsake regularly assembling together with the whole. Notice I used the word *regularly* instead of *routinely*. For many believers, worship is participated more so out of routine than out of a sincere desire to draw closer to God. This is evident by the number of people who are ill-prepared to worship. One of the keys to having a Spirit-filled encounter with God is proper preparation. Believers who don't prepare to worship, have prepared to fail in having meaningful Spirit-led worship. When believers saturate their minds with worldly music and conversation on their way to the house of God, how can they really hear from heaven in worship? Others have partied the night away and then come to the house of God looking for a comfortable place to drift

---

[19] Hebrews 10:25.

off into a state of restfulness while saying I went to church. Eutychus,[20] whose name means fortunate, probably wasn't the first person to fall asleep in church and he certainly won't be the last. If believers prepare privately, when they gather publicly, then they have positioned themselves to enjoy a Spirit-filling worship experience.

Reflectively, private and corporate worship cannot be separated. They are intertwined with the Holy Spirit as the binding Agent. Corporate experience is empowered by personal experience. But, personal experience needs affirmation and interpretation in corporate worship.[21]

Corporate worship is important to believers because they receive strength from one another and are able to help one another on the **Power walk**. Not surprisingly, many do not fully appreciate the importance of corporate worship. Surveys have revealed that on any given Sunday, at even the most vibrant churches in the United States, twenty-five percent of the congregation is absent. Some absences are due to illnesses, work-related responsibilities, or family vacations and reunions. However, there is a large percentage of absences that are due solely to two factors: neglect of obligation or laziness.

One of Satan's smartest tricks is to convince believers that they do not need to go to the house of God. Not only is it important to the new believer, but every believer should

---

20 Acts 20:9.

21 Marvin E. Tate article on Worship, Butler, p. 1421.

want to be in the presence of other individuals with similar thoughts and beliefs. "Enter into His gates with thanksgiving and into His courts with praise. Be thankful unto Him and bless His name."[22] Thanksgiving and praise are two of the defining reasons that believers come together. Another forgotten reason is the solace that can be found among believers.[23]

Corporate worship is important. But you don't have to take my word for it; let's see how Jesus viewed worship. The Bible recalls that whenever Jesus entered a new town, on the Sabbath, He would make His way to the synagogue. Therefore, if corporate worship was good enough for Jesus, even while being pursued by His enemies, who are we to question God's commandment to assemble ourselves together? There are going to be times that the believer's spirit will be willing, but due to the rigors of the day, the flesh will be weak. In these moments of exhaustion, rely on the Holy Spirit to provide the necessary "get up and go." For those who still might make the excuse that home worship is all a believer needs, God calls us to worship in His sanctuary. The Bible tells us that "Hezekiah sent to all Israel and Judah and wrote letters also to Ephraim and Manasseh, that they should come to the house of the Lord at Jerusalem, to keep the Passover unto the Lord God of Israel."[24] In an effort to worship, "many people shall go and say, Come ye, and let us

---

22 Psalm 100:4.

23 Psalm 42.

24 2 Chronicles 30:1.

go up to the mountain of the Lord, to the house of the God of Jacob . . ."[25]

In your effort to progress spiritually, believers must rely on the power of the Holy Spirit to teach them how to worship and to be guided through worship. **Worship** becomes truly meaningful when it involves a partnership between the believer and the Holy Spirit. When this partnership is in place and the believer has asked the Holy Spirit to direct the worship experience, then and only then will the believer know what it means to worship Him in Spirit and in truth.

Several years ago I was an avid bass fisherman. My constant dream was to catch a trophy bass to hang on the wall. The most likely way to be in the right place to catch such a fish would have been to hire a professional guide, which I didn't, and to this day my wall is still bare. The guide's livelihood was directly dependent on being able to put people "on fish." His expertise came from spending many hours on the lake and documenting weather conditions and patterns of the bass. By putting your trust in him, you improve your odds of catching that trophy fish, although the outcome is not guaranteed. To worship God "in spirit and in truth", the believer must put his trust in the Great Guide, who is the Holy Spirit. He is able to put the believer's mind, body and soul in the right "position" whereby true worship can occur. To rely on self is to not enjoy the activating presence of the Holy Spirit, and as a result, our worship experience will be found lacking.

---

[25] Isaiah 2:3.

As you continue on your **Power walk**, you will find there are many obstacles, hurdles and bumps that will get in your way. The path is filled with obstacles like family, friends and acquaintances, hurdles like careers, clubs and caution, and bumps like pleasures, addictions and disinterest. I cannot be the only one who has lived at one of those addresses! Satan will cause friends to dissuade you about really worshipping God. Satan will make you choose between being committed to your career or to worshipping God. Satan will attack you in the pleasurable recesses of your mind, while rocking you into a state of "non-worship." I need to let you know that it is hard to truly worship God "in spirit and in truth" while clinging to the cares of this life. **Worship** is a process and mindset. So, having the mind of Christ is mandatory. To experience a deep and meaningful worship experience, the believer must prepare for it. The believer must align his or her mind and heart with God, waiting expectantly on truly being in the presence of the Lord. Calvin Coolidge aptly said, "It is only when men begin to worship that they begin to grow."[26] In Spirit-led worship, believers should have moments of praise, thanksgiving, adoration, prayer and confession, but more importantly, they should rely on the Holy Spirit.

Without a doubt, to traverse all of the bumps in the road that the believer shall encounter, you must learn to worship and your worship must be "in spirit and truth" as led by the Holy Spirit. It is critically important that this third discipline of the **POWER** acrostic—**Worship,** be taken seriously. In

---

26 Sloan, p. 67.

their book *A Life That Matters*, Joanne Sloan and Cheryl Wray closed the chapter on worship with these words, "Because God is Spirit, our worship of Him cannot be confined to a building. It must spill over into the entire world, impacting the lives of those around us with the life-changing message of God's love."[27]

True worship is the by-product of a Spirit-filled life. Therefore, believers must commit themselves emotionally, mentally and willfully to allow the Holy Spirit to initiate their private and corporate worship. By relying on the Holy Spirit, believers will be driven toward a closer relationship with God and at the same time their footing will be firm as they continue their **Power walk**.

---

[27] Ibid, p. 69.

## TIPS FOR MEANINGFUL WORSHIP

- Read prayers of worship in the Bible such as 1 Chronicles 29:11
- Read the Book of Psalms, keeping a spiritual eye open for psalms of worship. Some of these are Psalms 34, 96, 103, 111, 146, and 147.
- Learn how to worship God through praise and song.
- Before falling asleep at night, have a private worship service. Repeat a Bible verse, a praise song, or a favorite hymn. Don't forget to close the service with a period of prayer.
- Become a member of the praise and worship ministry. If none is available, mention it to your pastor and volunteer to spearhead the development of one.

# EVANGELIZE IN THE SPIRIT

"The fear factor keeps many Christians from being effective witnesses. When fear is taken out of evangelism, Christians get bold in sharing the Gospel."[28]

"And you shall receive power after the Holy Spirit comes upon you: and you shall be witnesses . . ." (Acts 1: 8).

I'd like to tell you a story about David. David was a man that had it going on. He had fame, fortune, and a fabulous future. He was socially connected, financially comfortable, and politically aspiring. However, that all changed when he paid a visit to his physician for an annual check-up. He was told that he had a condition that was terminal. The physician told him that he did not know how long he had to live, but death was unavoidable. Immediately, David came to the realization that his fame and fortune could not change his future. The finality of the word *death* resulted in David becoming despondent, depressed, and disgusted.

David, trying to make the best of his desolate situation, joined a support group for people with this terminal disease.

---

[28] Sloan, p. 75.

He was stunned at the number of people that shared his death sentence. One evening, as he was leaving one of the meetings, he ran into a man who told him he knew a doctor that could heal him of his terminal disease. Not getting his hopes up, David went to visit the doctor and sure enough, the doctor told him he could cure him and any one else he brought to him. David, having made some close friends, went back to his support group and told everyone how he'd been cured and led them to this miracle working doctor.

David had been delivered from certain death and he could think of only one thing: to go tell those with the disease about the miracle working doctor. If you were David, what would you have done? Would you have kept the good news to yourself? Would you have tried to bottle up the cure and sell it to the highest bidder? Or would you have done like David, tell everyone about your good fortune?

Although the above story is from my imagination, it has heavenly meaning. By birth, we are all like David, sentenced to death by the terminal disease called *sin*. This disease is 100 percent fatal to all who have it "For the wages of sin is death . . ." (Romans 6:23). But, for those who have experienced the cleansing cure that brings life, wouldn't it be selfish of us to keep it to ourselves? Don't you think you should pass the information along that others might know and experience the life saving gift that is through Christ Jesus our Lord?

The fourth discipline of the **POWER** acrostic is the need to **Evangelize**, which is another word for witness.

This discipline, that some believe to be the exclusive work of specialists such as pastors and missionaries should be participated in by every child of God.[29] I have heard it said, "When it comes to evangelism, most believers are like the Arctic Ocean,—frozen over at the mouth."[30] In evangelism, the hardest thing for most believers to do is to open their mouths. Speaking to the specialist mentality, the woman at the well (John 4) was not a specialist, but a cleansed adulteress, and she told others where they could find the Living Water. The man laying by the pool of Bethesda (John 5) was not a specialist, but he went back to his homeland and told people how he was healed. The man who was born blind (John 9) was not a specialist, but told doubters " . . . one thing I know, that, whereas I was blind, now I see" (John 9:25). All three of these individuals wanted others to know about the Great Physician called Jesus Christ. They desired to spread the Good News. They were not theologically trained, but they had been spiritually changed. They were not eloquent in speech, but their simple message of their own deliverance, led people to Christ. They realized that their newfound freedom did not make them "better" than others, but "better-off" and they wanted to share that with other.

With eternity in our hands (Matthew 16:19), it is the responsibility of every believer to share the saving knowledge of Jesus Christ with others. George McCalep, in his book *Faithful Over A Few Things,* gives three

---

29 2 Corinthians 5:18-20.

30 Green, p. 124.

Christian superlatives that are noteworthy as it relates to the discipline of evangelism: (1) The greatest need of this day is for Christians who will witness for our Lord Jesus and live devoted lives for His honor and glory. (2). The greatest tragedy for a Christian would be to stand before Christ empty-handed at the judgment having lived in a world of lost sinners and never having brought one soul to Christ. (3). The greatest joy for a Christian is to be used to win another to Christ.[31] Like as with David, having found the cure, we should be compelled to tell somebody about what the Lord has done for you.

Evangelism is the active calling of every believer to share the message of grace through Jesus Christ. It is the Spirit-led communication of the gospel of the kingdom in such a way or ways that the recipients have a valid opportunity to accept Jesus Christ as Lord and Savior and become responsible members of His church. Simply stated, "Tell them your story!"

Stan Clark, a Mission Service Corps volunteer with the North American Mission Board, says, "Most of the time witnessing is sidelined by fear." Clark adds, "At every evangelistic training session, fear is mentioned as the greatest barrier to witnessing. Christians should not assume fear is God's way of telling them that witnessing is not their gift. Fear is natural, but it is the intention of God for believers to overcome it and share their faith with others."[32] "God has

---

[31] George O. McCalep, Jr., Ph.D Faithful Over A Few things, p. 78.

[32] McHenry, p. 86.

not given us the spirit of fear, but of power, and of love, and of a sound mind."[33] Since fear is not of God, it must be of another spirit inferior to the Holy Spirit, who is able to give us the strength that we need to witness. "But ye shall receive power after the Holy Ghost is come upon you . . ."[34] In fact, believers have "God's Dream Team—the Holy Word, the Holy Spirit, and His Holy People. The Holy Spirit empowers and precedes, the Holy Word convicts and compels, and the Holy People seek and tell."[35]

As believers depend on the power of the Holy Spirit to carry out their evangelistic calling, they will find themselves not only going out with *holy boldness*, but they will also feel themselves growing spiritually. Every time believers tell someone about what God has done in their lives, their personal assurance will grow.

Take for instance the man who was born blind, as previously mentioned. Caught between the "rock" of the doubters, and the "hard place" of Jesus Christ, he made a simplistic confession " . . . for I once was blind, but now I see." Every time he told his story, his faith would grow and the same will be true with the power walker.

You might be saying that I just started my Power walk, or there is so much to learn, how or where do I start? Those are valid questions, but remember, Evangelism is not about

---

33 2 Timothy 1:7 KJV.

34 Acts 1:8 KJV.

35 McCalep, p. 78.

what you can do, but about what God does through you by the power of the Holy Spirit. The heartbeat of the gospel message is simple. It is the story of the life, death, and resurrection of Jesus Christ. **Evangelism** is about telling that Jesus Christ is the only one who is able to save those who desire having Him in their lives. **Evangelism** is about God and His plan, love, and righteousness. **Evangelism** is about the lost souls of people that are in bondage. **Evangelism** is about Jesus and the Good News and not about us. And **Evangelism** is the responsibility of all believers, having been commissioned to "make disciples." Joe Aldrich reminds us that "unsaved people are not the enemy; they are victims of the enemy."[36]

As a believer, you have the power to evangelize, but you must not become paralyzed by fear. Yes, in one's evangelistic endeavors, there will be those who won't listen and others that might treat you harshly, but those responses are not reasons to give up. You must continue to sow seed, and "the seed is the Word of God."[37] As you go and sow, some seed will fall by the wayside, some upon the rock and some among the thorns, but some will also fall on good ground.[38] The farmer that has a bad harvest the first time does not stop sowing, but continues in anticipation of a coming harvest. As the believers involve themselves in evangelism, they must look at every *no* as an eventual *yes*, otherwise Satan will tempt them to quit. Forever keep in mind, just as you were, so are many others who are looking for the cure. Be it family

---

[36] McHenry, p. 85.

[37] Luke 8:11.

[38] Luke 8:6-8.

member, friend, neighbor, co-worker, or stranger, they are terminal and need to be introduced to the Great Physician and as His ambassador, you are commissioned to do just that. The thought of being a co-laborer with Christ in bringing the offer of salvation to mankind should be exciting for the believer. As a Power walker, you are now God's instrument to make a difference in the life of the lost and dying world.

How does God do this? By the power of the Holy Spirit. The Holy Spirit, who precedes, convicts, and regenerates the heart of the lost, is essential to success. Although it is good to have formulas and methodologies, success is not rooted in your abilities, but in His power. He empowers the believer to witness. He gives the believer wisdom. He grants the believer *boldness.* He helps in the believer's praying, while at the same time giving the believer the desire to see people saved.[39] However, models and methods are beneficial as you incorporate the discipline of **Evangelism** into your **Power walk**.

Models can be as simple as using one verse of Scripture to verbalize a before and after experience. Take the following verse as an example. "For the wages of sin is death, but the gift of God is eternal life."[40] With this verse, the believer can discuss the importance of being on the right side of the *but.* On the left side of the *but* is wages, sin and death, while on the right side we have the gift, God and eternal life. The one

---

39 Reid, p. 160.

40 Romans 6:23.

necessity that moves people from the left to the right is the Gospel of Jesus Christ.

There are many other evangelistic tools that a believer can use. Some of them are mentioned below.

The first evangelistic tool is the ABC outline:

- *Admit* to God that you are a sinner and then repent (Romans 3:23; 3:10-18).
- *Believe.* By faith receive Jesus Christ as God's Son and accept Jesus' gift of eternal life (John 3:16).
- Confess your faith in Christ as Savior and Lord (Romans 10:9-10).

A second tool is the FAITH acrostic:

- **F** *is for forgiveness.* We must have God's forgiveness for our sins (Ephesians 1:7).
- **A** *is for available.* Forgiveness is available for all (John 3:16).
- **I** *is for impossible.* It is impossible for God to allow sin into heaven (Romans 3:23).
- **T** *is for turn.* Turn means repent, turn from sin and turn to God (Romans 10:9).
- **H** *is for heaven.* Heaven is eternal life (John 14:3).

A third tool is the Roman Road model:

- "For all have sinned and come short of the glory of God" (Romans 3:23).
- "But God commendeth his love toward us, in that while we were yet sinners, Christ died for us" (Romans 5:8).

- "For the wages of sin is death; but the gift of God is eternal life through Jesus Christ our Lord" (Romans 6:23).
- "That if thou shalt confess with thy mouth the Lord Jesus, and shalt believe in thine heart that God hath raised him from the dead, thou shalt be saved. For with the heart man believeth unto righteousness; and with the mouth confession is made unto salvation" (Romans 10:9-10).

A fourth tool that could be used is the more in depth Continuing Witness Training Model Presentation.[41] As you can see, there are many ways to introduce people to Christ, so as the Spirit leads you to people, take the time to find out where they are, both mentally and spiritually, and what they are thinking. Using tact, something that many believers are short on, establish a common ground and go from there. Adapt the message to the moment. Be willing to change the method, but never compromising the message. For example, Jesus, the master communicator, never dealt with any two people exactly the same way. The woman at the well had spent a lifetime trying to fill her void with men while Nicodemus (John 3) tried to fill his void with theology. Theology won't deliver anybody, but the God of theology will. Establish a relationship with the person, then based on your discoveries, make your connection there. Let the Holy Spirit guide your words, and help you build a bridge between the person's need and the simple message of the gospel.

---

[41] North American Mission Board. Continuing Witness Training Model Presentation (4200 North Point Parkway, Alpharetta, GA 30022-4176). See Appendix III for the complete presentation.

Believers are to be co-laborers in the gospel with Christ, and they are able to perform their tasks effectively by depending on the power from the Holy Spirit. In this **Power walk**, it is declared that we shall receive power *after* the Holy Spirit is come upon you. The *after* is crucial to the success of our evangelistic work. I can remember my mother saying "Son, *after* you have finished your homework, then you can go outside and play." I can hear the employer tell an employee, "*After* you have completed the said assignment, then you will be considered for promotion." I can hear the coach, the leader, the pastor, the friend, the husband or wife say "*After* you have done "this", then you will be able to do "this." God operates the same way in relations to your ability to evangelize effectively. Having received Jesus Christ as Lord and Savior, He, the Holy Spirit, takes up residence within you and gives you the power to evangelize. It was because of the indwelling of the Holy Spirit that one message was preached and three-thousand souls came into the knowledge of God. It was because of the indwelling of the Holy Spirit that Stephen told the Good News even though he lost his life.

While on this **Power walk**, believers must be confident that God has equipped them to tell others about the saving grace of Jesus Christ. Believers must not fret if the recipient of the evangelism rejects the message from God. Simply offer up a prayer for the person and move to the next individual that the Holy Spirit directs you toward. The response to the Good News might be varied; the heart of the person might be hard, shallow, contaminated or receptive;[42] but remember God gives the increase through the power of the Holy Spirit.

Evangelism is a ministry of *show and tell.* Believers must show others the Jesus in them by letting "[their] light so shine before men that they might see [their] good works and glorify [their] Father which is in heaven."[43] Believers must tell others about the Jesus who saved them: "For God so loved the world that He gave His only begotten Son, that whosoever believeth in Him should not perish but have everlasting life."[44]

Only the Holy Spirit can take a willing witness and a seeking sinner and bring them together. It was the Holy Spirit that brought Philip and the eunuch together.[45] This chance encounter, in man's eye, lead the eunuch to hear the Word, to be convicted by the Word, to believe the Word, and to be converted into the faith. Every believer has some divine appointment with his or her name on it if he or she would be sensitive to the leading of the Holy Spirit.

Evangelism is experienced more than it is learned. It is not a promotion that uses gimmicks, seems coercive or focuses on numerical success. Evangelism is a passion of love that has the reward of joy and exhilaration, and is most effective when the believer relies on the leading of the Holy Spirit to convict and to convert.

---

42 Matthew 13:18-23.

43 Mathew 5:16.

44 John 3:16.

45 Acts 8.

By evangelizing, the believer continues to make spiritual progress and is drawn into a more excellent relationship with the Lord. The responsibility is not to "just do it," but to do it in the power of the Holy Spirit.

## EVANGELIZE: JUST DO IT!

- Ask God for daily witnessing opportunities.
- Attend an evangelism class or seminar to become a more effective evangelist.
- Write down five names of people you know are not Christians. Begin to pray for them daily and ask God to give you the opportunity to share your faith with them.
- Become proficient at using one of the witnessing tools that have been mentioned in this book.
- Make a commitment to witness to your non-Christian family members. One way to do this is to schedule a family time to watch the *Jesus* film.
- Read biographies of people whose lives have been transformed through the love of Christ (John Wesley, Dwight Moody, Billy Graham, and others).
- Make certain that your *audio*, what you say, and your *video*, what you do, match your witness.

# READ IN THE SPIRIT

"There is only one possible way to grow strong spiritually—reading and studying the Word of God.[46]

"For whatever things were written aforetime were written for our learning, that we through patience and comfort of the scripture might have hope."[47] "All scripture is given by inspiration of God, and is profitable for doctrine, for reproof, for correction, for instruction in righteousness."[48]

Thomas Jefferson served as president of the Washington, D. C. School Board during his tenure as President of the United States. One of his duties on the school board was to select textbooks to be used by the students. He selected the Bible as the primary text with the following rationale: "I have always said, and always will say that the studious perusal of the sacred volume will make us better citizens."[49]

---

46 Sloan, p. 43.

47 Romans 15:4.

48 2 Timothy 3:16.

49 McHenry, p. 24.

I concur with President Jefferson, and I add that the systematic and sincere studying of the word of God will equip, train, and motivate the believer to make positive strides toward spiritual maturity. A familiar statement is that "reading is fundamental." As believers continue their **POWER walk**, reading the Word of God is essential. However, believers should not just be resolved to the act of reading simply for information, but for illumination and inspiration as well. As the believers read, they should do so relying on the power of the Holy Spirit to open up their hearts and minds to really hear what thus says the Lord. Just as the Word of God is the power unto salvation, so too is it a school master for spiritual growth. Therefore, by immersing oneself in the Word of God, the believer gains the mind of Christ and learns what it requires to be one of His disciples.

The fifth and final discipline of the **POWER** acrostic is **Read** the Word of God. With the acrostic in mind, this element will be viewed synonymously as studying, for the purpose of this book. Although the discipline of **Reading** doesn't automatically translate to the discipline of study, you can do the former without taking part in the latter, reading is a part of studying. If believers are to grow spiritually, then they must read the Word of God with their spiritual eyes and ears open to the visual and audible leading of the Holy Spirit.

The Bible is the greatest book ever written, the best-seller of all time. It is supernatural in its origin and inerrant in its structure. Although thousands of years have passed, it is still fresh and applicable today. The Bible fulfills every role and provides every need for and in our lives. The Bible is spiritual food for the nourishment of believers and is the standard that everything should be evaluated against. It shapes the lives, thoughts, attitudes and actions of believers. The Bible provides believers with much needed information about the Person of God. Likewise, it furnishes them with the plan for salvation and functions as a tool for witnessing. It strengthens believers with the hope they need to face uncertainty with faith and courage and the divine instruction that is profitable for maintaining uprightness on the **Power walk**. In short, the Bible is God's instruction manual of life and a "how to" book on developing a personal and everlasting relationship with Him. Not to read and meditate on the Word of God leads to spiritual suicide. Unfortunately, there are those that subject themselves to just such a painful and unnecessary death.

George Gallup once said: "Although people revere the Bible, they don't read it."[50] According to a survey by Tyndale House Publishers, 64 percent of Americans don't read the Bible. W. James Russell said, "Although the value system of the United States and Western civilization is based on the Judeo-Christian ethic, surveys indicate fewer than 17 percent of the American people read the Bible regularly. We are trying to sustain a value system with little or no knowledge of the historically proven truths of our biblically established value system."[51] If believers are to become better Christians, they must first become students of the Bible. Doing so will result in growth that will be rooted in facts and not in fantasy.

---

50 Sloan, p. 42.

51 Ibid, p. 42.

Before proceeding with our discussion on the importance of reading the Bible, it is imperative that proper hermeneutical principles be understood. *Right* reading is more important than *just* reading. Although the word *hermeneutics* might be foreign to many, simplistically it describes that practice or discipline of interpretation, which is something we do whether reading a book, the newspaper, or a letter written by a friend. The reader seeks to determine what is the intent of the author. If one reads with the pretense that the Bible can mean whatever the reader interprets it to mean, de-contextualization, taking a passage out of context, could occur. Some schools of thought will say this is acceptable behavior, but I did not graduate from one of those schools. It is my belief, which is in agreement with many theologians, that Scripture can never mean what the author did not initially intend for it to mean. The meaning of a passage of scripture originates and is historically locked with the author. Although scripture can have multiple implications, it can only have one meaning, that of the author. In other words, a passage of scripture can never mean what the original author never intended it to mean. Robert Stein, in his book *A Basic Guide to Interpreting the Bible*, states "What the text meant when it was written, it will always mean. It can no more change than any other event of the past can change, because its meaning is forever anchored in past history."[52] Reading the Bible without regard to historical, hermeneutical, contextual, or exegetical rules, invalidates one's interpretation,

---

52 Robert, H. Stein. A Basic Guide to Interpreting the Bible (Grand Rapids, MI: Baker Books, 1994), p. 26.

no matter how accurate it might sound. It is through accurate interpretation that right application can be modeled.

Continuing with our discussion of the fifth discipline, the psalmist declares: "Wherewithal shall a young man cleanse his way? By taking heed thereto according to thy word."[53] He goes on to say "I will delight myself in thy statutes: I will not forget thy word."[54] In this, the longest of the Psalms, the psalmist goes on to say, "Thy word is a lamp unto my feet and a light unto my path."[55] If believers don't read the "map of the gospel," how can they expect to see the spiritual booby traps that Satan has laid in their way? To walk safely in the woods at night, we need a light so we do not trip over tree roots or fall into holes. While on the **POWER walk**, believers will walk daily through a dark forest of evil, and therefore, they will need to know where and where not to step. The Bible should be the believer's light that guides the way, for the Bible reveals the entangling roots of temptation, the counterfeit value of vices, and the fallacious philosophies of man. Believers must read and study the Bible in order to see clearly and to stay on the right path. **Reading** the Word of God should be done repeatedly, prayerfully, carefully, contemplatively, imaginatively, purposefully and obediently and with eyes, mind and heart opened to what the Holy Spirit has to say. Richard Foster says it should be done "repetitively, with much concentration, comprehensively and reflectively."[56]

---

53 Psalm 119:9.

54 Psalm 119:16.

55 Psalm 119:105.

56 Foster, pp. 64-66.

All believers should make it a priority to read the word of God and to meditate on it daily. Through the act of meditation, believers call upon the power of the Holy Spirit to magnify the scripture and to bring all things that they have read to remembrance.[57]

One of the primary reasons for reading the Word of God is to find out what God has planned for them, which should be a priority for all believers. "All scripture is given by inspiration of God, and is profitable for doctrine, for reproof, for correction, for instruction in righteousness: That the man of God may be perfect, thoroughly furnished unto all good works."[58] The Word of God is the ultimate all-purpose cleaner. The Word of God cleans, disinfects and deodorizes, but the Word also delivers. As believers **Power walk** toward spiritual maturity, they can find hope in the Word of God.[59] The believer's goal should be to become like the Berean believers who were more noble than those at Thessalonica. This pronouncement was not made out of favoritism, but because "with readiness of mind, [Berean believers] searched the scriptures daily."[60]

God through His Spirit was the inspirational force for the entire Bible. That Scripture is "given by inspiration" refers not to the way God inspired its writing, but to the source of the Bible's content. In the Greek, "given

---

57 John 14:26.

58 2 Timothy 3:16,17.

59 Romans 15:4.

60 Acts 17:11.

by inspiration" comes from *theopneust*, meaning it was "*God-breathed.*" The idea that Paul was making in using the phrase "God-breathed," according to R. C. Sproul, was that "it was an idea of expiration, not inspiration; that the Bible is *breathed out* by God."[61] Because it is God-breathed and trustworthy, believers should read it and apply it to their lives because it carries with it the authority of God. The Bible is the standard for testing everything else that claims to be true. By reading what God has provided, the believer has a safeguard against false and satanic doctrine; and a source of guidance for continuing the **POWER walk**.

Again from the *MasterLife Discipleship Training*, Avery Willis says that to grow in the Word, believers must "hear the Word, examine the Word, analyze the Word, remember the Word, and think on the Word.[62] We will analyze a portion of this statement shortly, but as one looks closely at the key points: hear, examine, analyze, remember, and think, using the first letter of each word, the acrostic **HEART** is formed. Believers must make every effort to hide the Word of God in their *heart* that they might not sin against Him.

This acrostic is supported by the Word which believers are instructed to read.

- Hear— "If any man have ears, let him hear" (Mark 4:23).

---

61 Sproul, Five Things Every Christian Needs To Grow, p. 13.

62 Willis, pp. 177,178.

- Examine— "Blessed is he that readeth, and they that hear the words of this prophecy, and keep those things which are written therein: for the time is at hand" (Revelation 1:3).
- Analyze— "These were more noble than those in Thessalonica, in that they received the word with all readiness of mind, and searched the Scriptures daily, whether those things were so" (Acts 17:11).
- Remember— "Wherewithal shall a young man cleanse his way? By taking heed thereto according to thy word.
  Thy word I hid in my heart, that I might not sin against thee" (Psalm 119:9,11).
- Think— "Finally, brethren, whatsoever things are true, whatsoever things are honest, whatsoever things are just, whatsoever things are pure, whatsoever things are lovely, whatsoever things are of good report; if there be any virtue, and if there be any praise, think on these things." (Philippians 4:8).

Believers must realize, at the heart of spiritual growth is the ability to hear and apply the Word in their life and behind this application of the Word is the Holy Spirit. Returning to the HEART acrostic, let's look at 2 Timothy 3:16,17 analytically to appreciate the spiritual richness it has for maturing believers. Within this passage, believers are reminded that Scripture is profitable for four things. It is profitable for doctrine, reproof, correction, and instruction in righteousness.

• The Bible tells us what is right: " . . . profitable for doctrine.":

- "My doctrine shall drop as the rain, my speech shall distil as the dew, as the small rain upon the tender herb, and as the showers upon the grass" (Deuteronomy 32:2).
- "For I give you good doctrine, forsake ye not my law" (Proverbs 4:2).
- "If thou put the brethren in remembrance of these things, thou shalt be a good minister of Jesus Christ, nourished up in the words of faith and of good doctrine, whereunto thou hast attained" (I Timothy 4:6).
- "Holding fast the faithful word as he hath been taught, that he may be able by sound doctrine both to exhort and to convince the gainsayers" (Titus 1:9).

In school, the teacher provides each student with rules that are to be followed. These rules spelled out what was allowed within the classroom. God is no different. He has provided the believer with "rules for holy living", the Holy Bible, and as they are followed, the believer's **Power walk** is not marred by that which is "unholy."

- The Bible tells us what is not right: " . . . for reproof.":

- "For the vile person will speak villainy, and his heart will work iniquity, to practice hypocrisy, and to utter error against the Lord, to make empty the soul of the hungry, and he will cause the drink of the thirsty to fail" (Isaiah 32:6).
- "Beware lest any man spoil you through philosophy and vain deceit, after the tradition of men, after the rudiments of the world, and not after Christ" (Colossians 2:8).

- "Be not carried away with divers and strange doctrine. For it is a good thing that the heart is established with grace; not with meats, which have not profited them that have been occupied therein" (Hebrews 13:9).

Likewise, that same teacher gives students some rules that showed them what was off limits. To cross the line was to place oneself in harm's way. God, our Father, who desires nothing more than to keep His children out of harm's way, has provided some similar rules. As believers read the Word of God, they will happen upon some practical imperatives, "Thou shalt not's" and it is important that believers adhere to them.

- The Bible tells us how to get right: " . . . for correction.":

- "Blessed is the man whom thou chastenest, O Lord, and teachest him out of thy law" (Psalm 94:12).
- "My son, despise not the chastening of the Lord; neither be weary of his correction. For whom the Lord loveth he correcteth; even as a father the son in whom he delighteth" (Proverbs 3:11,12).
- "As many as I love, I rebuke and chasten: be zealous therefore, and repent" (Revelation 3:19).

At times believers will stray from the "way that is right" seeking the "way that appears right" and the Lord will have to chasten them. The correction that God brings is not out of hate, but out of love. When you were growing up how many times did you hear your parents say to you "I'm whipping you because I love you" or better yet "This hurts me more than it hurts you." God is faithful in all His dealings and just in all His ways, and, therefore, out of love He corrects us to bring us back into obedience.

• The Bible tells us how to stay right: " . . . for instruction in righteousness.":

- ♥ "Trust in the Lord, and do good; so shalt thou dwell in the land, and verily thou shalt be fed" (Psalm 37:3).
- ♥ "Commit thy way unto the Lord; trust also in him; and he shall bring it to pass" (Psalm 37:5).
- ♥ "It is better to trust in the Lord than to put confidence in
- ♥ man" (Psalm 118:8).
- ♥ "Trust in the Lord with all thine heart and lean not unto thine own understanding. In all thy ways acknowledge him, and he shall direct thy path" (Proverbs 3:5,6).
- ♥ "Trust ye in the Lord for ever: for in the Lord JEHOVAH is everlasting strength" (Isaiah 26:4).

As I mentioned earlier, you do not have to teach a child how to do wrong, but he or she must be taught how to do right. "Instruction in righteousness" is not an overnight sensation but a continuous determination of programmed instruction. The Word of God is not haphazard in nature, but a beautifully woven masterpiece of literary genius, with God as the Ultimate Writer. If believers aren't to drift back into the life that they were delivered from, they must "put to death" the old man, through the Word of God.

This passage of Scripture has inspired me to read the Bible looking for these four profitable things. In your own study, it would be beneficial to read the Bible with four different colored highlighters in hand. When you come across each profitable item, highlight it for future reference with a different color. This color coded system will be helpful as you continue on your **Power walk**.

For those on the **Power walk**, reading the Word of God should lead to being made "perfect, thoroughly furnished unto all good works."[63] And this perfection will be accomplished as believers rely on the power of the Holy Spirit. Some spiritual hurdles will be hit on the **Power walk**, but with the Holy Spirit's assistance, fewer will be hit as the believer gets closer to the **Power walk** finishing line.

As believers read the Word of God, the Word will activate all of the other disciplines of the **POWER** acrostic. The more believers give themselves to reading the *God-breathed* Word, the more Spirit-filled their prayer lives will be. The more believers read the *God-breathed* Word and allow the Holy Spirit to direct them, the easier it will be to obey. The more believers read about worship in the *God-breathed* Word, the more effective and efficient they will be in worship toward God. The more believers learn about witnessing from the pages of the *God-breathed* Word, the more willing they will be to evangelize. The Word of God is given by inspiration, and is therefore worthy of meditation. When the Word has worked itself into the soil of the believers soul, through

---

63 2 Timothy 3:17.

meditation, the Holy Spirit will cause its germination,[64] resulting in steady maturation.[65] Having relied on the Holy Spirit to assist in the above mentioned process, the natural progression is to become involved in replication.[66]

If believers are to become assets and not liabilities to kingdom building, then they must **Read** the Word and rely on the Holy Spirit for interpretation. Reading is fundamental in almost every aspect of our lives, but *reading* the word of God is essential to spiritual growth and for continuing your **POWER walk**. An old adage is true when it comes being successful on the **Power walk**, if we emphasize only the Word, we dry up. If we emphasize only the Spirit we blow up. But, when we marry the two, we grow up.

---

[64] 1 Peter 2:2 "As newborn babes, desire the sincere milk of the word, that ye may grow thereby."

[65] 1 Corinthians 13:11 "When I was a child, I spake as a child, I understood as a child, I thought as a child: but when I became a man, I put away childish things."

[66] Matthew 28:19,20 "Go ye therefore, and teach all nations, baptizing them in the name of the Father, and of the Son, and of the Holy Ghost: teaching them to observe all things whatsoever I have commanded you: and, lo, I am with you always, even unto the end of the world."

## READ THE BIBLE FOR ALL ITS WORTH

- Purchase a Study Bible that best meets your individual needs. Seek guidance from your pastor or a Christian friend.
- Devote a part of the day for reading the Bible without interruption.
- Read through the Bible during the year, if you have not done so.
- Keep a journal of the spiritual truths that God reveals to you as you read.
- Participate in Bible study groups at your church or in community Bible studies.
- If able, take the Old and New Testament survey classes at a local Bible college or university.
- Develop a system that works for you to help you memorize Scripture.
- Commit to memory one Scripture verse per week.

## HELPFUL BIBLE STUDY BOOKS


- Arthur, Kay. *How to Study the Bible.* Eugene, OR: Harvest House Publishers, 2001.
- Fee Gordon D., and Douglas Stuart. *How to Read the Bible for All Its Worth.* Grand Rapids, MI: Zondervan, 1981, 1993.
- Sproul, R. C., and Robert Wolgemuth. *What's in the Bible.* Nashville: Word Publishing Group, 2001.
- Stein, Robert H. *A Basic Guide to Interpreting the Bible.* Grand Rapids, MI: Baker Books, 1994.

# SUMMARY

In conclusion, the key disciplines to having a Spirit-led **POWER walk** are:

- **PRAY IN THE SPIRIT**: "The Lord is near to all who call upon him, to all who call upon him in truth" (Psalm 145: 18).
- **OBEY IN THE SPIRIT**: "But be ye doers of the word, and not hearers only, deceiving your own selves" (James 1: 22).
- **WORSHIP IN THE SPIRIT**: "God is Spirit: and they that worship him must do so in spirit and in truth" (St. John 4: 24).
- **EVANGELIZE IN THE SPIRIT**: "And you shall receive power after the Holy Spirit comes upon you: and you shall be my witnesses . . ." (Acts 1: 8).
- **READ IN THE SPIRIT**: "For whatever things were written for our learning, that we through patience and comfort of the scripture might have hope" (Romans 15:4).

**POWER UP! TAP INTO HIM TODAY!**

# EPILOGUE

As a Christian, through the power of the Holy Spirit, you have everything you need to be what you should be. Spiritual progress is not a process of gaining things that you did not have when you became a believer, but developing that which was put in you at conversion. When you were born in Christ, through the power of the Holy Spirit, you were made spiritually whole and have all you will ever need to become mature—you have the Holy Spirit. However, Christians can short-circuit their progression by trying to participate in the **Power walk** without the aid of the **Power** within. If your joy, peace, and hope are to become full and you are to reach perfection, then it must be accomplished "through the Holy Spirit."[67] Furthermore, to grow and become spiritually mature, I encourage you to unite with a Bible-based church whereby you can be taught the many doctrines of the Word of God by a Spirit-filled pastor. "[The Lord] will give you pastors according to [His] heart, [who] shall feed you with knowledge and understanding."[68] My recommendation is not denominationally based, but biblically based. The search should begin with prayer. Then the church

---

[67] Romans 15:13.

[68] Jeremiah 3:15.

should be a learning, loving, worshipping, and evangelistic congregation. Don't settle for anything less.

Although you might be able to intellectualize the Power walk, you will never be able to fully internalize it without the Holy Spirit as your Coach. **Prayer, Obedience, Worship, Evangelism, and Reading** the Word of God will only be religious activities that will yield marginal growth until you tap into the power that comes only through the Holy Spirit. He is the one that will help the power walker experience the explosive growth God desires.

On your **Power walk**, you will encounter some tracks that are fast, slow, rough, or smooth, but each track condition can be overcome with the heavenly assistance of the Holy Spirit. **Prayer, Obedience, Worship, Evangelism, and Reading** the Word of God are spiritual disciplines that you must willingly and faithfully incorporate into you daily life. These disciplines will help you on your spiritual journey and relying on the power of the Holy Spirit makes your Power walk both relational and fruitful. You will notice a transformation in your actions, words, and deeds. Having put your trust in God and faith in Jesus Christ, you must call upon the power of the Holy Spirit to guide you on your **Power walk**. In closing, I encourage you as a fellow Power walker to "be steadfast, unmovable, always abounding in the work of the Lord, forasmuch as you know that your labor is not in vain in the Lord."[69]

May God bless you richly as you take your **POWER walk**!

---

[69] 1 Corinthians 15:58.

# APPENDIX I

## POWER WALK CHECK-UP
## A QUICK CHECKLIST TO EVALUATE THE BELIEVER'S SPIRITUAL PROGRESS ON THE POWER WALK

1. Do you constantly rely on God?
2. Are you working hard to please God?
3. Are you really obeying God?
4. Are you learning from the Bible?
5. Are you practicing what you learn?
6. Have you given up in the difficult areas?
7. Is the character of God manifesting itself in you?
8. Do you love your fellow believers?
9. Do you love your enemies?
10. Are you winning against the *flesh*?
11. Are you resisting Satan in the Spirit's power?

"God wants you to be a victor, not a victim; to soar, not to sink; to overcome, not to be overwhelmed." How are you doing in your **POWER** walk?

# APENDIX II

**Continuing Witness Training Model Presentation**
**North American Mission Board**

**F.I.R.E.**

Family
[Do you have any children, spouse, etc.?]]

Interests
[Do you have any hobbies?]

Religious Background
[When you attend church, where do you go?]]

Exploratory Questions
[Can I ask you a couple of questions?]

a. Have you come to a place in your life that you know for certain that you have eternal life and that you will go to heaven when you die?

[The Bible says, . . . (1 John 5:13). Now I know for certain I have eternal life and when I die I will go to heaven. Let me ask you another question.]

b. Suppose you were standing before God right now and He asked you, "Why should I let you into my heaven?" What do you think you would say?

[God loves us and has a purpose for our lives. The Bible states it this way,. . . (John 3:16). God's purpose is that we have eternal life.]

**GOSPEL**

A. God's Purpose

1. We receive eternal life as a free gift (Romans 6:23).
2. We can live a full and meaningful life right now (John 10:10).
3. We will spend eternity with Jesus in heaven (John 14:3).

[As I searched for real meaning in life, I discovered that my sinful nature kept me from fulfilling God's purpose for my life.]

B. Our Need

1. We are all sinners by nature and by choice (Romans 3:23).
2. We cannot save ourselves (Ephesians 2:9).
3. We deserve death and hell (Romans 6:23).

[God is holy and just and must punish sin, yet He loves us and has a provided forgiveness for our sin. Jesus said, . . . (John 14:6.]

## C. God's Provision

1. Jesus is God and became man (John 1:1,14).
2. Jesus died for us on the cross (1 Peter 3:18).
3. Jesus was resurrected from the dead (Romans 4:25).

[The only way for Jesus to affect our lives is for us to receive Him. The Bible says, . . . (John 1:12).]

## D. Our Response

1. We must repent of our sin (Acts 3:19).
   a. Repentance is not just feeling sorry for our sin (Acts 26:20).
   b. Repentance is turning away from our sin and turning to God through Jesus.
2. We must place our faith in Jesus (Ephesians 2:8).
   a. a. Faith is not just believing facts about Jesus (James 2:19).
   b. b. Faith is trusting Jesus.

3. We must surrender to Jesus as Lord (Romans 10:9,10).
   a. a. Surrendering to Jesus as Lord is not just saying we give our lives to Jesus (Matthew 7:21).
   b. b. Surrendering to Jesus as Lord is giving Jesus control of our lives.

[As evidence of giving Jesus control, we will want to identify with Him. The New Testament way is to confess Jesus publicly and to follow Him in baptism and church membership.]

**Leading to a Commitment**

## A. Commitment Questions

1. Transition Question: "Does what we have been discussing make sense to you?"
2. Willingness Question: "Is there any reason why you would not be willing to receive God's gift of eternal life?"
3. Commitment Question: "Are you willing to turn from your sin and place your faith in Jesus right now?"

## B. Clarification—To receive Jesus you must:

1. Repent of your sin.
2. Place your faith in Jesus.
3. Surrender to Jesus as Lord.

[Let's bow our heads, and I will lead in prayer.]

## C. Prayer

1. Prayer of Understanding
2. Prayer of Commitment
3. Prayer of Thanksgiving

**Immediate Follow-up**

# BIBLIOGRAPHY

Butler, Trent C. *Holman Bible Dictionary.* Nashville, TN: Holman Bible Publishers, 1991

Dahl, Gordon. Life Walk. May/June 1991.

Foster, Richard J. *Celebration of Discipline*. New York, NY: HarperCollins Publishers, 1978.

*Franklin Holy Bible Electronic King James Version*, Bookman II Model KJV-1440.

Burlington, NJ: Franklin Electronic Publishers, 1999.

Green, Michael. *Illustrations for Biblical Preaching.* Grand Rapids, MI: Baker Book House, 1989.

Laurie, Greg. *New Believer's Guide to Effective Christian Living*. Wheaton, Ill: Tyndale House Publishers, Inc, 2002.

McCalep, George O. Jr., PhD. *Faithful Over A Few Things.* Lithonia, GA: Orman Press, 1996.

McHenry, Raymond. *McHenry's Quips, Quotes & Other Notes*. Peabody, MA: Hendrickson Publishers, 1998.

North American Mission Board. *Continuing Witness Training Model Presentation.* 4200 North Point Parkway, Alpharetta, GA 30022-4176 Piper, John. *Let the Nations be Glad!* Grand Rapids, MI: Baker Book House, 1993.

Reid, Alvin. *Introduction to Evangelism.* Nashville, Tennessee: Broadman & Holman Publishers, 1998.

Ryrie, Charles C. *The Holy Spirit*. Chicago, IL: Moody Press, 1965.

Sloan, Joanne Stuart, and Cheryl Sloan-Wray. *The Life That Matters*. Birmingham, AL: New Hope Publishers, 2002

Sproul, R. C. *Five Things Every Christian Needs To Grow*. Nashville, TN: W Publishing Group, 2002.

Sproul, R. C. *Following Christ*. Wheaton, IL: Tyndale House Publishers, 1996, c1991.

Spurgeon, Charles. *Holy Spirit Power*. New Kensington, PA: Whitaker House, 1996.

Stein, Robert, H. *A Basic Guide to Interpreting the Bible.* Grand Rapids, MI: Baker Books, 1994.

Steinmetz, Sol, ed. *Random House Webster Dictionary*. New York: Random House, 1993.

Thompson, Frank Charles. *The Thompson Chain-Reference Bible*. Indianapolis: B. B. Kirkbride Bible Co., 1988

Thrasher, William L. Jr. *Basics for Believers*. Chicago, IL: Moody Press, 1998. Willis, Avery T. Jr. *MasterLife—I Discipleship Training*.

Wood, Charles R. *Sermon Outline on Spiritual Renewal*. Grand Rapids, MI: Kregel Publications, 1969.

# ABOUT THE AUTHOR

Born in Port Arthur, Texas, Rev. James Edward Webb is the son of the late Virginia Wright and the grandson of the late Emmaline Horton. He is married to Sharon Lavern, and they have two children, Donavon James and Carmen LaJoyce. The couple and their children reside in Longview, Texas. Rev. Webb earned the Bachelor of Arts Degree in economics from the University of Texas in Austin and the Certificate in Ministry and Christian Leadership at East Texas Baptist University in Marshall, Texas.

Rev. Webb serves as the senior pastor of the Bethesda Missionary Baptist Church of Marshall, Texas. Prior to him accepting this position, Rev. Webb served as the Youth Minister at the Mount Olive Missionary Baptist Church of Longview, Texas for three years.

Rev. Webb is the past president of the Unity Fellowship Ministry of Marshall and currently serves as the president of the Congress of Christian Education for Texas Educational Baptist State Convention.

Rev. Webb has written several Discipleship Training Guides, including "Church Etiquette," "Let's Talk About Sex!: A Biblical Perspective," and "Justification, Sanctification & Glorification: The Three Fold Principle," just to name a few.

Rev. Webb's hobbies are collecting baseball, basketball and football cards, golfing and reading.